The UK & The Euro

The UK & The Euro

Paul Temperton

JOHN WILEY & SONS, LTD
New York • Chichester • Weinheim • Brisbane • Singapore • Toronto

Other Wiley Editorial Offices

John Wiley & Sons, Inc., 605 Third Avenue,
New York, NY 10158-0012, USA

Wiley-VCH Verlag GmbH, Pappelallee 3,
D-69469 Weinheim, Germany

John Wiley & Sons Australia, Ltd, 33 Park Road, Milton,
Queensland 4064, Australia

John Wiley & Sons (Asia) Pte Ltd, 2 Clementi Loop #02-01,
Jin Xing Distripark, Singapore 129809

John Wiley & Sons (Canada) Ltd, 22 Worcester Road,
Rexdale, Ontario M9W 1L1, Canada

British Library Cataloguing in Publication Data

A catalogue record for this book is available from the British Library.

ISBN 0 471 49955 2

Edited, designed, illustrated & typeset in 10.5pt Palatino by Nick Battley, London,
England (http://www.nickbattley.com).

Cartoons: Dave Thompson

Printed and bound in Great Britain by Antony Rowe Ltd., Chippenham, Wiltshire.

This book is printed on acid-free paper responsibly manufactured from sustainable
forestation, for which at least two trees are planted for each one used for paper
production.

To Emily and Freddie

For a happy and prosperous future: with or without the euro

Contents

Preface

Whether or not to 'join the euro' is, without doubt, one of the most significant issues facing the UK. If the UK did join, the changes would be far-reaching and significant. No one would be unaffected.

The UK will not join unless the move is approved in a referendum. This is likely to take place in the next few years.

It is the aim of this book to present, in a balanced way, the issues which are relevant to those seeking guidance on how to vote in such a referendum.

I hope it succeeds in that purpose.

P.T.
Chalfont St Giles, Buckinghamshire
March 2001

Acknowledgements

Thanks go, first and foremost, to my wife, Nicky, for her excellent comments on the various drafts of the book.

Peter Coë and Kim and Neal McTier also provided very valuable comments on the early drafts.

Sally Smith and her colleagues at John Wiley and Sons, Ltd. provided great support and encouragement for the book.

Nick Battley produced this book, as he did my other books in this area, with speed and efficiency.

William Ledward provided very valuable help on the history of sterling, the gold standard and the break-up of previous monetary unions.

The contributors to the first and second editions of *The euro* (published by Wiley in 1997 and 1998, respectively), which I edited, must also be thanked. Those two books provided valuable background for this publication.

Since 1997 I have delivered many seminars, presentations, speeches and training programmes on the euro. I have also acted as a consultant to a wide range of organisations. These activities have taken me to 26 different countries and exposed me to a wide range of views on the euro. I thank the many people I have come across in these travels. They have been instrumental in determining the choice of material to cover in this book.

As always, any errors remain entirely my own responsibility.

P.T.

1

Introduction

The aim of this book is to provide an insight into the issues surrounding whether or not the UK should 'join the euro'. If it does join the euro, the UK would become a member of the 'euro-area' or 'eurozone'. This is currently a group of twelve countries – Austria, Belgium, Finland, France, Germany, Greece, Ireland, Italy, Luxembourg, the Netherlands, Portugal and Spain. For these countries the first step towards introducing the euro was taken by fixing the value of their currencies to the euro. For example:

$$€1=1.95583 \text{ Deutschemarks}$$

This conversion rate came into force on 1 January 1999 and means that there is equivalence between Deutschemarks and euros. It is a *conversion* rate not an *exchange* rate. It is fixed permanently – it will not change – and it is legally binding. It is expressed to six significant figures and must be used in precisely that form when converting: no shortening or simplification of the conversion rate is allowed. It means that converting from Deutschemarks to euros is like converting from pints to litres or from miles to kilometres. This is the single most important feature of the euro and most of the consequences of 'joining the euro' stem from it.

Since the conversion factors were set it has been possible to operate in either the old national currencies or euros. The extent of the switchover has varied between different sectors of the economy. The financial markets switched over to the euro at the earliest opportunity. There was a 'changeover weekend' from 31 December 1998 to 3 January 1999 during which the foreign exchange market and most of the bond and equity market 'redenominated' amounts from national currency to euro. Several large companies also switched over to the euro at an early stage. They have used the euro in presenting their accounts, in invoicing and in some of their banking transactions. But until euro notes and coins come into circulation in 1 January 2002 the changeover cannot be complete.

The three-year period between the euro's legal formation and the introduction of euro cash was a necessary preparatory stage. In particular, most of that time was needed in order to mint the 60 billion new euro coins and print the 14.5 billion new euro banknotes.

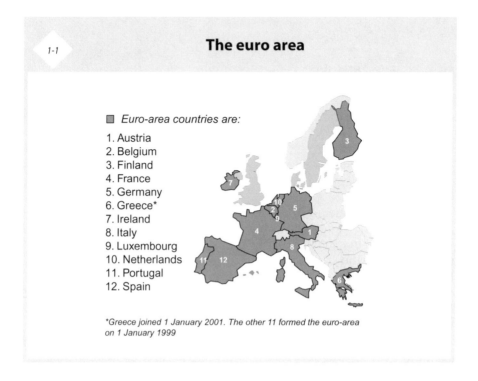

The euro area

1-1

☐ *Euro-area countries are:*

1. Austria
2. Belgium
3. Finland
4. France
5. Germany
6. Greece*
7. Ireland
8. Italy
9. Luxembourg
10. Netherlands
11. Portugal
12. Spain

*Greece joined 1 January 2001. The other 11 formed the euro-area on 1 January 1999

The absence of euro notes and coins in this period was undoubtedly a deterrent to more widespread use of the euro. Credit and debit card payments, payments by cheque, standing order and direct debit in euro were all possible from 1 January 1999. But take-up of euro-denominated bank accounts by the public was very limited. Most preferred to wait to the last minute before changing over.

If the UK decides to join the euro its preparatory phase may be simpler and shorter. The euro will already be in circulation in the eurozone and many in the UK will have been 'exposed' to the euro. But that does not mean that the UK could join the euro 'overnight'. A series of decisions has to be made in the UK and by the EU before the UK can join. In total, the overall switchover – incorporating the length of time to decide and prepare – will probably take between three and five years.

As with the founder countries, the UK would have a conversion factor between the euro and sterling. For example:

$$€1=£0.798635$$

This would probably be in place for around two years before sterling notes and coins were replaced by euros. Most of the significant *economic* consequences of joining the euro stem from this fixing of sterling's value. A range of other consequences does, of course, follow from the complete replacement of sterling with the euro.

The structure of the book

Exchange rate 'fixes' are, of course, nothing new for the UK. There have been many in the past: to the value of gold, to the dollar and to other European currencies. Indeed, the starting point of this book (Chapter 2) is a review of the exchange rate fixes that have been used in the past: why they were used, the problems that were encountered and why, eventually, each failed.

The creation process of the euro was a complex one and in many respects the switchover from sterling to the euro for the UK would be more straightforward. The way in which the euro was created – and in particular the construction of the conversion rates – is explained in Chapter 3. This is a chapter for those with a fondness for technical detail. It can safely be skipped by anyone happy enough to take for granted that a six significant figure conversion rate would link sterling to the euro if the UK chose to join.

We then turn to the main advantages and disadvantages of the UK joining the euro, in Chapters 4 and 5. The main advantages (Chapter 4) are identified as exchange rate stability, the ability to compare prices across different countries more easily (helping to produce lower prices), a more efficient operation of the EU's single market, better functioning financial markets and (possibly) lower interest rates. The main disadvantages relate to the 'one size fits all' approach to interest rates that will be adopted across the euro-area, the inflexibility of the exchange rate and the consequent loss of control over two of the most important levers of economic policy. The transition costs of moving to the euro will also be substantial.

Before the UK applied to join the euro, it would need to pass two sets of tests, which are discussed in Chapters 6 and 7. These will only be relevant if the Labour government is re-elected for a second term of office as the Conservatives have a 'keep the pound' pledge.

The first set of tests are Gordon Brown's 'five tests' of whether joining the euro is in the best interests of the UK. The European Union has a different set of tests, based on the so-called 'convergence requirements' that are discussed in Chapter 7. Both sets of tests will need to be passed before the UK can join. But even these tests are not as comprehensive as many would like. In particular, neither addresses the issue of the exchange rate at which the UK joins. Given that joining the euro means that the rate of sterling against the euro will be locked permanently, it is important to get it right. Assessment of the 'right' exchange rate is the subject matter of Chapter 8. A range of other considerations, which is not covered by the two sets of tests, is discussed in Chapter 9.

Joining the euro would mean that the European Central Bank (ECB) would set interest rates for all of the countries in the euro area. Thus, responsibility for determining UK interest rates would no longer rest with the Bank of England. The significance of this change is discussed in Chapter 10.

Given the uncertainties surrounding the UK joining the euro, a timetable is a little difficult to pin down. We emphasize the interaction of three timetables: of the sequence of decisions in the UK; the sequence of decisions in the EU and the length of time needed to prepare.

Living with the euro, but still being outside the euro-area, is an option that is discussed in Chapter 13. If the UK did join, many would still want an exit route if it all goes wrong. We discuss whether such an exit is feasible in Chapter 14. Chapter 15 sets out some conclusions.

2

A short history of sterling's exchange rate

The first step involved in the UK joining the euro is fixed permanently in value to the euro. Although such a fix would undeniably be a major event, it would not be unprecedented – indeed, for most of the last three hundred years, sterling's value has been either fixed, or at least closely linked to, the value of something else, be it gold or another currency. Indeed, *not* having some form of linkage – as has been the case since sterling left the European Exchange rate Mechanism in 1992 – is the exception rather than the rule.

In this chapter we look at the various exchange rate fixes that have been employed in the past, and ask:

- how they worked when they were in operation;

- why some lasted for many years whereas others were abandoned after a relatively short time; and

- what these experiences can teach us about the issues surrounding the UK 'joining the euro'

Isaac Newton & the Gold Standard

1717-1931

The first period in which sterling was fixed began in 1717. At that time, the money in circulation in the UK consisted mainly of gold and silver coins. However, over time, the quality of the coinage underwent significant change.

There were two main problems:

First, up until the seventeenth century, coins were struck by hand – with the result that they were not uniform in either size or weight. This made them susceptible to 'clipping', that is to say, having their edges trimmed. The clippings that were collected in this way were then melted down to provide an illicit, but lucrative, income for those involved. While the clipped coins retained their face value, their *intrinsic value* – that is to say their value in terms of the gold or silver content – was clearly reduced.

Second, the intrinsic value of the coinage was further undermined by the state itself, which increased the alloy content and correspondingly reduced the gold and silver content. This practice was most widespread under the spendthrift Henry VIII.

Various monarchs – Henry's daughter Elizabeth I being one of them – made attempts at 'recoinage' to re-establish the value of sterling. However, these efforts met with only limited success since the coins continued to be struck by hand, and were thus still susceptible to clipping. Furthermore, there were periodic, and acute, shortages of coins; and public acceptability of those in circulation was often limited.

Thomas Gresham, a financier during the period of Queen Elizabeth's recoinage, established a new approach to the problem when he formulated 'Gresham's Law', which states that 'bad money drives out good'. This law can be demonstrated as follows: Suppose you have a choice between using two coins to make a payment, both with a face value of one pound sterling. One has a high gold content and shows no signs of clipping, while the other contains more alloy and has clipped edges. Which do you use for making the payment and which do you keep? Gresham stated – not surprisingly – that the 'bad money' would be used for making payments whereas the good quality money would be kept out of circulation.

An improvement in the situation began on Christmas Eve 1663 when Charles II issued a warrant for the creation of new gold coin – the guinea – to be struck from gold imported from West Africa. The new coin was a great success. Mechanical production ensured its uniformity; and the inscription *DECUS ET TUTAMEN* around its edge proved a major deterrent to clipping. This same Latin inscription – meaning 'ornament and safeguard' – currently appears on UK one pound coins.

A more comprehensive recoinage took place between 1695 and 1696. Mechanically-produced silver coins were newly minted and issued, with clipped coins being taken in exchange. Sir Isaac Newton, who became Warden of the Mint just as the recoinage programme began, subsequently became Master of the Mint and took on the task of determining the precise value of the pound sterling in relation to gold. This process involved determining the quantity of gold in one pound sterling (or, more precisely, in the one guinea coin, as this was the principal gold coin in circulation). After lengthy deliberation, and particular attention paid to the gold content of similar continental European coins, Newton finally established the relationship as one pound sterling being equal to 113.0016 grains of gold – that is to say, just under one quarter of an ounce. Alternatively, one standard ounce troy of gold was deemed equal to £3 17s 10½d. (Before decimalization in 1971 there were twenty shillings (s) per pound and 12 pence [denoted by the letter 'd' from denarius, an ancient Roman coin] per shilling.).

Isacc Newton discovers the gold standard

There is a parallel here with the current issue of the conversion factors between national currencies and the euro. It is often claimed that the six significant figure conversion factors will be difficult to understand and therefore be an obstacle to public acceptance of the euro. But if the Georgians could manage with complex conversion amounts, surely the scale of the current problem should not be overstated?

With only a few wartime interruptions, this parity between the value of the pound sterling and gold was retained for more than two hundred years. Britain adopted a formal gold standard in 1816, largely as a result of the sudden abundance of the metal. More gold was mined in the 19th century than in the preceding 5,000 years. Thus, use of gold coins (rather than silver and copper) became the norm. Thus, the gold standard was more accurately a 'gold coin' standard, since although notes which represented, and were redeemable into, gold were in circulation, gold coin was the principal form of cash . European countries followed the UK onto the standard in the 1870s. The US, meanwhile, maintained a bimetallic (gold/silver) standard until 1900, as did India. China maintained a silver standard. Nevertheless, by the end of the 19th century, most of the world's industrialized nations shared the gold standard

The fixed parities between each country's currency and gold meant that the exchange rates between the world's major currencies were also fixed.

For example:

In England, one gold sovereign (£1), which had replaced the guinea as the main gold coin in 1821, was defined as equal to 113.0016 grains of gold (Sir Isaac Newton's conversion rate).

£1 = 113.0016 grains

In the US, one dollar ($1) was equal to 23.22 grains of gold.

$1 = 23.22 grains

Thus

£1 = 113.0016 ÷23.22 = $4.8666

Similar calculations for all the other currencies on the gold standard meant that there was a set of fixed exchange rates between all the main trading countries in the world. This stability of exchange rates is widely credited with helping to generate the boom in international trade in the late nineteenth and early twentieth century.

With the outbreak of the First World War, Britain unofficially left the gold standard in 1914 (and officially in 1919). In 1925, largely at the insistence of the then chancellor of the exchequer, Winston Churchill, the UK adopted a gold bullion standard in 1925. The bullion standard reflected the demise of gold coin in circulation (although notes could be redeemed for 400-ounce bullion bars). The real problem, though, was the adoption of the pre-war traditional price of gold (and, by extrapolation, the same fixed exchange rate with other currencies, notably the dollar).

During the War, prices in the UK had risen more sharply than in the US. By adopting the bullion standard at the same fixed exchange rate with the US dollar, this meant that goods produced in the UK were correspondingly more expensive than those in the US, thus putting UK exporters at a serious disadvantage. One way of correcting the problem would have been for prices and wages in the UK to fall, making the UK

2-1   **Fixing sterling's exchange rate**

1717-1931

Type of system:	Gold standard
Fixed to:	Gold
Period of 'fix':	214 years
Main reasons for demise:	Fixes were suspended during and immediately after wars. General breakdown of gold standard in the 1930s

1931-1946: Sterling not subject any fix or linkage

1946-1949

Type of system:	Bretton Woods system
Fixed to:	US dollar at US$4.03/£
Period of 'fix':	3 years
Main reasons for demise:	Post-war dollar shortage; desire to improve UK competitiveness

1949-1967

Type of system:	Bretton Woods system
Fixed to:	US dollar at US$2.80/£
Period of 'fix':	18 years
Main reasons for demise:	Sterling crisis caused by large trade deficit

1967-1972

Type of system:	Bretton Woods system
Fixed to:	US dollar at US$2.40/£
Period of 'fix':	5 years
Main reasons for demise:	General breakdown of world fixed exchange rate system. US suspension of convertibility of dollars into gold.

1972

Type of system:	The 'Snake'
Fixed to:	Other European currencies in the Snake
Period of 'fix':	6 weeks
Main reasons for demise:	General exchange market turmoil

June 1972-March 1987: Sterling not subject any fix or linkage

Mar 87-Mar 88

Type of system:	Deutschemark cap
Fixed to:	Deutschemark - 'cap' of DM3.00/£
Period of 'fix':	1 year
Main reasons for demise:	Overheating UK economy

Oct 87-Sep 92

Type of system:	ERM membership
Fixed to:	Deutschemark - range of DM2.78-DM3.13
Period of 'fix':	2 years
Main reasons for demise:	ERM problems due to German reunification
	Recession in UK economy

September 1992 onwards: Sterling not subject any fix or linkage

once again competitive with the US. However, slashing wages is not a political option – attempts to do just that led to the General Strike of 1926 and attendant widespread social unrest. With UK exports remaining uncompetitive, and demand for imports strong, the UK started to run a large balance of payments deficit.

In theory, adoption of the gold standard provides an 'automatic' form of adjustment in such circumstances. In the UK, the balance of payments deficit is 'paid for' by running down gold reserves. With lower gold reserves, the supply of money – which is backed by gold – is reduced. This will force either prices to fall or demand in the economy to contract. In the countries receiving the UK's gold, the opposite happens: an increase in their gold reserves allows an increase in the money supply, leading to stronger demand and higher prices.

The mechanism has, however, seldom worked in that manner. The theoretical mechanism is, by its very nature, slow to operate. Furthermore, the relationship between gold flows and the supply of money becomes less rigid when paper money takes on greater importance (as it did when the Bank of England became the sole note issuer after 1844) and, indeed, when the banking sector assumes greater importance.

In practical terms, the 'policy options' the UK faced in the late 1920s are virtually the same as those available to any modern-day nation wanting to maintain a fixed exchange rate in the face of a balance of payments deficit. These are:

- *Monetary Policy*
  Raise interest rates, in order to reduce demand in the economy and cut imports. Higher interest rates will also attract capital to the UK, helping to finance the deficit.

- *Fiscal Policy*
  Increase taxes or reduce government spending, also to reduce demand and cut imports.

If these fail to correct the problem, or if the government lacks the stomach to pursue the policies vigorously enough, then the currency can be devalued – either voluntarily or out of necessity.

The massive scale of gold and capital outflows in 1931 left the UK with little option but to leave the gold standard. Other countries followed suit – the US in 1933, then Belgium and France. For each country, the intention was to cheapen the cost of their exports, thereby boosting economic growth and employment. Of course, if every country tries to pursue the same policy, the exercise becomes futile. In modern terminology, this action is described as a 'competitive devaluation' and over the years, many countries have been accused of trying to kickstart their economies by taking such measures. For example, following their crisis is 1997-1998, the maintenance of extremely weak currencies by Asian emerging economies was seen as an attempt to gain competitive advantage. Similar accusations were levelled at the UK in the mid-1990s as sterling fell to low levels against other European currencies.

Back in the 1930s, this so-called 'beggar thy neighbour' policy of seeking devaluation was adopted by so many countries that it led directly to the renowned period of global depression

Bretton Woods

1946-1971

Partly as a result of the experience of these competitive devaluations in the 1930s, a fixed exchange rate system (based on gold) was reintroduced after the Second World War. This was the 'Bretton Woods' system, named after the New Hampshire town where the meetings to establish it took place. Under this system, implemented in 1946, each country pledged to maintain a fixed exchange rate between its currency and either the dollar or gold. Since one ounce of gold had a fixed value of $35, whether the currency was fixed to either gold or the dollar was largely immaterial. Under the system, the Deutschemark was set equal to1/140 of an ounce of gold, meaning it was worth $0.25 ($35/140).

This system of fixed exchange rates was supported by a new organization, the International Monetary Fund (IMF), the function of which remains largely the same to this day. In particular, the IMF provides foreign exchange to countries if their exchange rate parity comes under pressure. A country's ability to borrow from the IMF is determined by its 'quota' – essentially the amount of money it subscribes in order to become a member of the IMF. The condition of obtaining an IMF loan is that the country implements IMF-approved policies – usually involving restrictive monetary and fiscal measures – to support its currency.

The main burden of adjustment is still placed on the country with the balance of payments deficit – as it was under the gold standard. This has often been criticized as a weakness of the system, with some claiming that just as much adjustment should take place on the part of the 'creditor country'. This view is typified in the current pressures for Japan – with a consistently strong current account surplus – to adopt policies to encourage demand in its economy, thereby sucking in imports.

Under the Bretton Woods system, restrictions were placed on the extent of the convertibility between currencies and gold. In the US, for example, only central banks were allowed to convert dollars into gold. Exchange rates could be adjusted in the case of a fundamental trade deficit, but such adjustments or devaluations were intended to be – and in practice were – relatively infrequent.

In the UK, the introduction of the Bretton Woods system meant that maintaining the fixed exchange rate was the central aim of UK economic policy. The policy got off to a bad start, however, with a post-war balance of payments deficit forcing sterling to be devalued by 30% just three years after the system was established.

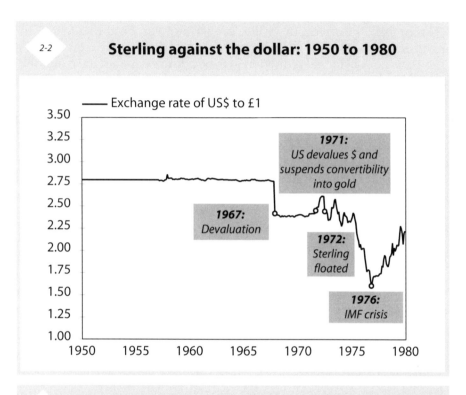

2-2

Sterling against the dollar: 1950 to 1980

2-3

Sterling against the dollar: 1980 to 2001

From 1949, however, the value of sterling was fixed at $2.80/£ for eighteen years. Despite a long period of restrictive domestic policies, there was no substantial reduction in the trade deficit, with the result that sterling was once again devalued in 1967 – from $2.80/£ to $2.40/£. The prime minister of the day, Harold Wilson, addressed the nation on a Sunday afternoon, his speech containing the supposedly reassuring phrase that the value of "the pound in your pocket" had not been devalued. In the words of Philip Ziegler, 'Wilson became stamped as the man who pretended that devaluation would not affect the buying power of the pound; worse still the one who tried to pass off devaluation as a triumph instead of the economic defeat that it was.'

However, the UK was not the only country experiencing problems with its trade deficit. A mounting deficit, coupled with sharply rising inflation, was also behind President Richard Nixon's announcement (on 15 August 1971) that the dollar was to be devalued against gold and that convertibility between the dollar and gold, even for central banks, was to be terminated. This marked the end of the Bretton Woods system. In December 1971, under the 'Smithsonian Agreement' – the successor to Bretton Woods – the dollar was devalued to 1/38 of an ounce of gold and other currencies were revalued against the dollar. However, attempts to set new fixed rates proved difficult, and the world officially turned to floating exchange rates in 1973.

An experiment with a Snake

1972

The turmoil surrounding the breakdown of the Bretton Woods system saw the UK's first attempt to link sterling's value to that of other European currencies. The idea of monetary union in the EEC had been launched in the Werner report of 1970. In the early months of 1972 the four major currencies – the Deutschemark, sterling, French franc and Italian lira – were joined by a number of minor currencies in forming the so-called 'Snake'. Each country in the group had the individual responsibility of keeping its currency in line with the others in the system. This group then moved together, as a block, against other world currencies such as the dollar. However, with foreign exchange markets remaining volatile, and no agreement between the European countries on mutual currency support, the system soon fell apart. Sterling was a member of the Snake for only six weeks and as from 23 June 1972 sterling was officially 'floated'.

Floating in theory, sinking in practice

1972-1976

Following the breakdown of the link between the dollar and gold in 1971, sterling initially appreciated against the US dollar, but the trend proved to be short-lived. Fuelled by expansionary monetary and fiscal policies, as well as the effects of the oil price hikes, UK inflation rose sharply in the mid-1970s.

The slide in sterling's value accelerated in 1976, with the currency falling below $2 to the £1 in the spring, and to a low point of $1.60 in October. The UK approached the IMF for a loan to shore up the value of sterling.

The IMF crisis

1976 & 1977

The condition of the loan was the UK signed a 'Letter of Intent' in which it pledged to pursue stable economic policies, involving a reduction of the government's budget deficit, and control of monetary and credit growth.

The IMF-induced policy shift meant that managing the exchange rate was less of a priority, although it was not completely abandoned. Sterling appreciated strongly after the implementation of the IMF plan and an attempt was made to limit the appreciation of sterling's trade weighted index – its value against a basket of currencies. The government set a relatively narrow range for the trade weighted index, but the policy was abandoned in October 1977 when the scale of intervention needed to keep sterling's value *down* (!) was considered to be too great.

Mrs Thatcher's monetarist policies

1977-1987

A policy of controlling the growth of the money supply and domestic credit was, therefore, already in place before Mrs Thatcher came to office in 1979. However, the new Conservative government placed great emphasis of these monetarist approaches, and control of the exchange rate took a back seat for a while. Indeed, the tight monetary and fiscal

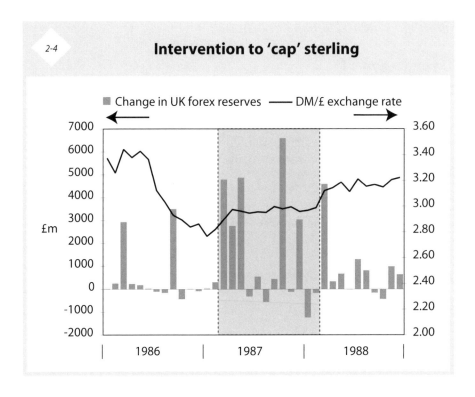

2-4

Intervention to 'cap' sterling

■ Change in UK forex reserves   —— DM/£ exchange rate

£m

1986   1987   1988

policies pursued by Mrs Thatcher's government contributed to a sharp, albeit short-lived, appreciation of sterling's value in the late 1970s and early 1980s. In the US, meanwhile, tight monetary policies were also being pursued to keep down inflation. The high level of US interest rates attracted capital to the US and the dollar began a marked appreciation thus causing sterling to end its appreciation and once more fall against the dollar. Central banks, still mindful of their failure to intervene to manage exchange rates in the 1970s, initially tolerated the sharp increase in the US dollar's value but, by early 1985, the dollar was widely considered to have reached an extremely overvalued value. Finance ministers from the Group of Seven (G7) countries meeting at the Plaza Hotel in New York agreed to intervene to bring reverse the dollar's appreciation.

Such intervention continued, from time to time, throughout the following two years and, by early 1987, the G7 agreed that exchange rates were now at broadly the 'right' levels. (As we discuss in Chapter 8, what constitutes a 'right' level is determined by reference to various measures of relative prices and the competitiveness of different countries.) Accordingly, at their meeting at the Louvre, in Paris in February 1987,

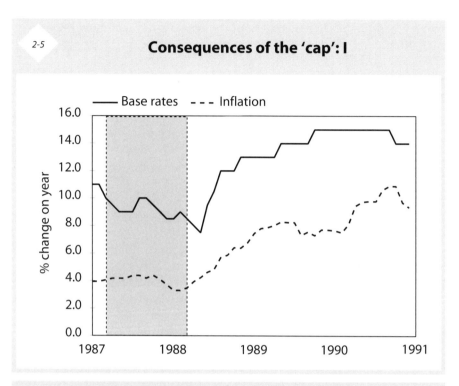

2-5

Consequences of the 'cap': I

Base rates — — — Inflation

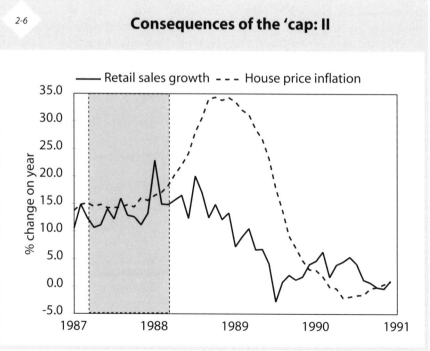

2-6

Consequences of the 'cap: II

Retail sales growth — — — House price inflation

they agreed to stabilise the value of the world's main currencies against each other.

Nigel Lawson's 'cap'

1987-1988

Nigel Lawson was chancellor of the exchequer at the time of the Louvre Accord and he used the Accord as the basis for his own attempt at stabilizing sterling's value. The policy chosen was to 'cap' the value of sterling against the Deutschemark at DM3.00/£, and not to allow sterling to appreciate above that level.

The main rationale for the policy was that it would ensure that, in the long term, UK inflation would fall into line with the inflation rate in Germany. The mechanism envisaged here was similar to that under the classical gold standard: with sterling and the Deutschemark tied together, competitive pressures would force prices and wages in the UK to rise no faster than those in Germany.

Soon after the policy was introduced, there were substantial inflows into sterling resulting in upward pressure on the currency, which soon came close to the DM3.00/£ cap. These flows of capital into the UK were encouraged by the UK's strong economic growth rate at the time – continental Europe, in contrast, was widely regarded as 'eurosclerotic', i.e. suffering from low growth, high unemployment and inflexible labour markets.

In order to keep sterling's value down, the Bank of England carried out massive intervention to buy foreign currencies and sell sterling. UK interest rates were also reduced. However, the UK economy started to show signs of 'overheating' – growing more strongly than its potential growth rate. Preventing an appreciation of sterling and reducing UK interest rates were precisely the wrong policies to follow in such circumstances.

One year after it was first introduced, the DM3.00/£ cap was removed and sterling was allowed to rise in value. By that time, however, inflationary pressures in the economy had built up substantially. Consumer spending was rising extremely rapidly and the housing market was booming. To rein in the inflationary pressures, there was a need to increase short-term interest rates, and they were duly hiked to reach a level of 15% by the end of 1989. However, the result was spectacular, as both the property market and consumer spending collapsed. By early 1990, the UK was in recession.

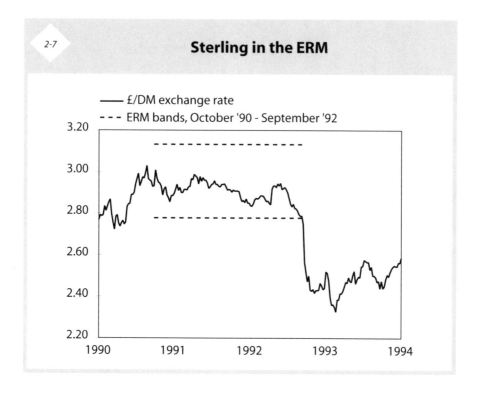

Sterling in the ERM

2-7

—— £/DM exchange rate

- - - ERM bands, October '90 - September '92

ERM membership

1990-1992

Ironically, John Major, who had taken over from Nigel Lawson as chancellor of the exchequer in October 1989, considered that joining the European Exchange Rate Mechanism was one of the best routes to secure lower UK interest rates. With a rationale similar to that for the DM3.00/£ cap, it was thought that UK rates would fall towards the German level if sterling was linked to the Deutschemark in the Exchange Rate Mechanism. German interest rates, at the time the UK joined in October 1990, were just over 8%, almost half the UK level.

UK interest rates did indeed fall after the UK joined the ERM, and continued to fall throughout 1991 and into 1992. But, as UK interest rates fell very close to the German level, further reductions in interest rates became more difficult to achieve. In the ERM, German interest rates had typically set the 'benchmark' for interest rates in all other ERM countries and it was virtually unknown for other countries' interest rates to fall

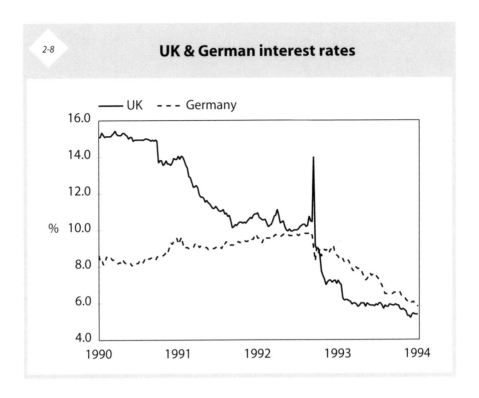

2-8

UK & German interest rates

below those in Germany. The main reason being that Germany had a long and well-established track record of low inflation.

The fact that the UK remained stubbornly stuck in recession meant that the British government wanted further interest rate reductions in order to stimulate the economy. The UK was not alone: France also wished to cut interest rates, but it too was effectively prevented from doing so because its levels were already very close to those in Germany.

Germany was suffering, however, from the inflationary pressures stemming from reunification, which had led to a large increase in government borrowing, a rapid expansion of the growth of money and credit in the economy, and a rise in inflation. In order to stem these inflationary pressures, German interest rates were heading higher, rather than lower, in the late summer of 1992.

The UK's problems were compounded by the fact that sterling had entered the ERM in 1990 at what was widely considered to be too strong an exchange rate against the Deutschemark, a view which, influentially, was also held by the Bundesbank, the German central bank. The clear conflict between what was needed in order to keep sterling in the ERM (higher interest rates), and what was needed to stimulate the UK economy (lower interest rates), reached breaking point in September

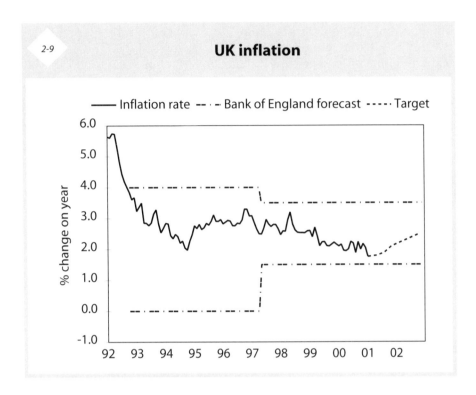

2-9

UK inflation

—— Inflation rate -- · - Bank of England forecast ····· Target

1992. On 16 September, with sterling at the bottom of the ERM's permitted band against the Deutschemark, the Bank of England was forced to intervene aggressively to support the pound. Foreign exchange speculators sold sterling, in the anticipation that the parity could not be held; George Soros, the fund manager, was reported to have made one billion dollars in profit by speculating against sterling on that fateful day.

The Bank of England was on the verge of running out of foreign exchange reserves when two increases in interest rates – first to 12% and then to 15% – were made in a vain attempt to support sterling. By the evening of 16 September, however, it was clear that the parity in the ERM could be held no longer and sterling withdrew from the ERM.

UK policy since leaving the ERM

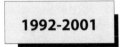

1992-2001

Since 1992, there has been no formal target, or link, for sterling's exchange rate – either against other European currencies or the US dollar. Instead, UK interest rates have been set with the intention of keeping the UK inflation rate within a 'target range'. In October 1992, this target range was initially set at zero to 4%, but was later revised to 2.5%, with a 1% band on either side, when the Labour government was elected in May 1997.

The inflation target has been met continuously since it was first set. This is quite a remarkable achievement given that the UK was been one of the most inflation-prone economies in the world in the 1970s and 1980s.

Joining the euro would necessarily entail significant changes, once more, in the conduct of UK monetary policy and the way in which UK interest rates are set. Amongst the most important changes are:

- The Bank of England would no longer decide on the level of interest rates for the UK economy. Rather, interest rates in the UK would be set at the common level of the euro-area.

- The governing council of the European Central Bank would decide the common euro-area interest rate. The ECB comprises a six-member executive committee plus the governors of each of the central banks of the euro-area (twelve currently, thirteen if the UK were to join).

- The current system, whereby the Bank of England's Monetary Policy Committee meets once a month in order to set interest rates for the UK economy would necessarily have to be abandoned.

Conclusions

For more than 250 years, up until the breakdown of the Bretton Woods fixed exchange rate system in 1972, the value of sterling was fixed either to gold or to the dollar. For the vast majority of the time, this 'fix' caused few problems for the economy, although there was always the option of changing sterling's value through a devaluation.

The 'normal' regime since 1972 has been for sterling to float against other currencies. At various times, however, sterling has been tied or linked in some way to other currencies. In particular, sterling was:

- linked to a group of other European currencies in the 'snake' (1972)
- 'capped' in terms of the value of its exchange rate index (1977)
- 'capped' against the Deutschemark (1987-1988)
- linked to other European currencies in the ERM (1990-1992).

All of these attempts at linking sterling's value have been abandoned after reasonably short periods of time. If there is one common thread that runs through the failures, it is that there was a conflict between the needs of UK domestic policy and those of maintaining the exchange rate.

For example, 'capping' sterling's exchange rate in 1987-88 led to interest rate cuts that fuelled an unsustainable boom in the economy. When sterling was in the ERM in 1990-1992, interest rates had to be kept higher than would be the case if purely domestic, UK conditions had been taken into account. This contributed to the depth of the recession.

Fixing sterling's value to the euro, and eventually replacing sterling with the euro, is an exchange rate fix which is 'tougher' than any of the exchange rate regimes of the past. There would be no way out: the step would be irreversible. Whether the UK economy is ready for such a step is the subject matter of the rest of this book.

3

The euro: an even briefer history

The euro came into existence on 1 January 1999. Euro cash – notes and coin – will come into circulation on 1 January 2002 and, after that, national currencies will be withdrawn from circulation quite quickly. The three-year gap between the formal, legal launch of the euro and its final introduction in the form of cash was necessary in order to provide adequate time for the 50 billion new coins to be minted and the 14.5 billion new banknotes to be printed.

In the three-year interim period, the euro has been used extensively in the financial markets and also by many large companies. However, use by small- and medium-sized companies, and the general public, has remained very limited. This situation will, of course, change in 2002 when notes and coin are introduced and bank accounts are converted from national or 'legacy' currencies into euro.

How the euro was created

The euro was created through two channels on the 1 January 1999. First, the euro replaced the Ecu, a basket of European currencies, on a 'one-for-one' basis. Second, each of the member countries of the euro-area adopted a fixed conversion factor between its own currency and the euro. Figure 3-2 provides details of the conversions.

Channel One: 'one-for-one' conversion with the Ecu...

In the Maastricht Treaty it was envisaged that the single European currency would be called the Ecu (European Currency Unit), but that it would change from being a basket of European currencies to be a currency in its own right. However, the name of the planned single currency was changed to the 'euro' at the Madrid summit in December 1995, when a set of measures were introduced to relaunch the single currency project.

3-1   1 January 1999: one Ecu became one euro and...

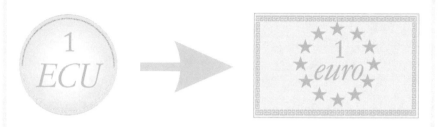

3-2   ...11 currency rates were irrevocably fixed to €1

1.95583	Deutschemarks	=
40.3399	Belgian francs	=
40.3399	Luxembourg francs	=
2.20371	Dutch guilders	=
1936.27	Italian lira	=
166.386	Spanish pesetas	=
200.482	Portuguese escudos	=
6.55957	French francs	=
0.787564	Irish punts	=
13.7603	Austrian schillings	=
5.94573	Finnish markka	=

...more recently, on 1 January 2001, Greece joined at a rate of GRD 340.750 to one euro

However, many contracts – particularly in the financial markets – had been previously drawn up in Ecu and the change of name led to some uncertainty as to whether Ecu contracts would become 'euro' contracts or, indeed, whether the new name set a precedent for breaking the contract. The issue was clarified, after substantial pressure from the financial community, in a European Council regulation in June 1997 which established that one Ecu became one euro.

The ECU itself was a 'basket' of European currencies, in the sense that it contained fixed amounts of 12 European currencies (see Figure 3-3).

Only nine of these twelve countries became members of the euro-area when it was launched. The UK and Denmark both 'opted out' of joining

3-3	**The Ecu**

Composition of the Ecu until 31 December 1998

=	0.6242	Deutschemarks
+	1.332	French francs
+	151.8	Italian lira
+	0.2198	Dutch guilders
+	3.301	Belgian francs
+	0.13	Luxembourg francs
+	0.008552	Irish punts
+	6.885	Spanish pesetas
+	1.393	Portuguese escudos
+	0.08784	British pounds
+	1.1976	Danish krone
+	1.44	Greek drachma

at that time, a facility that had been negotiated for each country and included in the Maastricht Treaty. Greece was excluded because it failed – in early 1998 – to meet the requirements for joining (although it subsequently met those tests in 2000 and was included in the euro-area as of 1 January 2001).

Complicating matters further, two countries that were not included in the Ecu basket, Austria and Finland, nevertheless became members of the euro-area. These two countries were excluded from the Ecu because they were not members of the EU, and hence not eligible for Ecu inclusion, when the Ecu's composition had last been revised in 1989.

This situation meant that, until 31 December 1998, Denmark, Greece and the UK continued to be included in the Ecu. As a result, fluctuations in these three currencies still affected the value of the Ecu right up until the time that the Ecu was transformed into the euro on 31 December 1998.

...and a set of fixed conversion factors

The second element of the euro's creation was the establishment of fixed conversion factors between each of the member currencies of the euro-area and the euro itself. Prior to the launch of the euro, the Exchange Rate Mechanism (ERM) linked together the currencies that were to form the euro. In the ERM, each currency had a central rate against every other currency in the mechanism, with a certain degree of fluctuation permitted from the central rates. Until 1992, these fluctuation bands had been quite narrow (plus or minus 2.25%, for most currencies) but they were widened in 1993 (to plus or minus 15%, for most currencies) after speculative pressures on the ERM.

Following the turbulence in European currency markets through 1992 and 1993, it took several years for inter-currency relationships to regain their stability. Indeed, in early 1995, there was a further crisis – albeit relatively minor – which was triggered by a devaluation of the Mexican peso (the so-called 'Tequila Crisis') but, soon after, the ERM finally achieved a degree of stability. A significant step in this return of confidence was the December 1995 Madrid Summit which, in addition to changing the name of the single currency, also reaffirmed the timetable set out in the Maastricht Treaty, i.e. the movement to monetary union no later than 1 January 1999.

Despite the 'success' of the Madrid Summit, there was still considerable uncertainty as to which currencies would actually join the single currency; and also the exchange rates which would form the linkage between the currencies.

The principal issue concerning the make-up of the euro-area membership stemmed from doubts over the ability of some countries to meet fully the Maastricht 'convergence criteria' (see Figure 3-4). Indeed, even at the late stage of end-1997, there was widespread expectation of a narrow monetary union, consisting of maybe five or six countries. In March 1998, however, the *Convergence Reports*, published jointly by the European Commission and the European Central Bank, recommended that no less than eleven countries should form the euro-area. These were: Austria, Belgium, Finland, France, Germany, Ireland, Italy, Luxembourg, the Netherlands, Portugal and Spain .

3-4   Convergence criteria for joining the euro

Inflation

The average consumer price inflation rate over the previous year must not exceed by more than 1.5 percentage points that of the three lowest inflation countries.

Government deficit

The planned or actual government deficit must not exceed 3 per cent of GDP, unless the ratio has been on a declining path and is approaching the 3 per cent level, or the excess is small and clearly temporary.

Debt stock

The gross general government debt must not exceed 60 per cent of GDP, unless the ratio is approaching 60 per cent at a satisfactory pace.

In assessing the two fiscal criteria, the medium-term economic and budgetary position of the member state and whether its deficit exceeds government investment may also be taken into account.

Exchange rate stability

A currency must have adhered to the normal fluctuation margins of the ERM in the two previous years without severe tensions. A member state may not have initiated a devaluation of its currency's central rate in the previous two years. Before the 1 August 1993 widening of ERM bands, 'normal fluctuation margins' were generally understood to be the 2.25 per cent bands, but 15% bands are now be considered 'normal'.

Bond yield

The average yield on long-term government bonds over the previous year must not exceed by more than 2 percentage points that on similar government bonds of the three lowest inflation countries.

This selection of countries was formally approved at a special European Council meeting in Brussels, which was convened in May 1998. The same meeting also announced that the central rates of the eleven countries in the Exchange Rate Mechanism would form the basis of their entry rates to the euro and thus the eleven countries' exchange rates settled on their ERM central rates in the final months of 1998.

To say that these two channels provided a tortuous route to forming the euro would probably be an understatement. Nevertheless, despite a complex pregnancy, the euro was born on time. The Ecu is consigned to the history books and the conversion factors between the euro and national currencies have become merely a matter of record. But what now?

Why has the euro been so weak against the dollar?

Since its launch, the euro has regularly made the news headlines. Much has been made of its apparent weakness, as it relentlessly fell in value, against other major currencies, such as sterling, the US dollar, the Swiss franc and the yen. Nevertheless, for the euro, it was the slide against the US currency that was crucial.

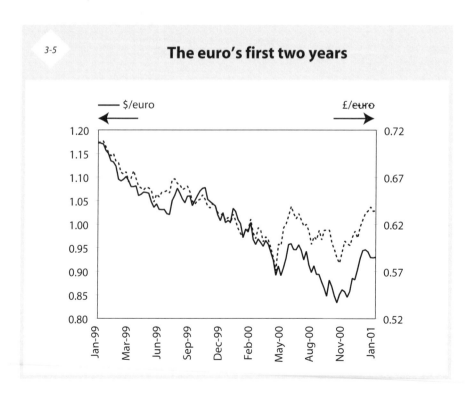

3-5

The euro's first two years

Figure 3-5 shows the euro's evolution against the dollar and sterling in its first two years. At the time of its launch in 1999, one euro bought $1.16, but that fell to a low point of just 82 cents in September 2000. So, why did the euro weaken so much?

Economists have no shortage of explanations – a fact which is particularly strange given their consensus view in 1998 that the euro would be a strong currency from birth! However, despite the wide range of 'excuses' for the weakness vis-à-vis the dollar, there are essentially four main factors behind the euro's poor performance: the trend in economic growth, the current account balance, capital flows and, last but not least, the difficulty in establishing confidence in a new currency.

The   collapsing   euro

Strength of the US economy; relative weakness in Europe

The US economy was very strong in 1999 and 2000 – far stronger indeed than anyone could have envisaged – and, naturally, the euro struggled against such a strong 'adversary'. However, going forward into 2001, this pattern looks set to change. The US economy is now slowing markedly while, in contrast, European growth is holding up relatively well. Most forecasters expect the eurozone to grow faster than the US in 2001 and this augurs well for the euro's relative strength.

The current account

The US is running a substantial current account deficit (4% of GDP in 2000, with the same expected again in 2001). In contrast, the euro-area's current account is in broad balance. In 2001, the eurozone should start to benefit from the delayed effects of the weakening of the euro, with increased export competitiveness. The US, meanwhile, is likely to suffer from the opposite effect, with the effects of the strong dollar continuing to work their way through to the export markets. The eurozone current account position is thus likely to strengthen further relative to the US, with a favourable knock-on effect for the euro's value.

Capital flows

Capital flows from the eurozone to the US were substantial in 2000, as European companies and investors were active in US acquisitions. Indeed, the one-way flow has been quite extraordinary. However, when the euro is finally launched as a day-to-day currency in January 2002, a wave of industrial consolidation is likely to take place across Europe, and the likelihood is that US companies will want to play a big part in that process. Clearly, if that turns out to be the case, capital flows from the US to Europe could become significant.

Similarly, portfolio flows from Europe to the US stockmarket have already started to slow now that the Nasdaq bubble has burst. Repatriation of funds and a growing emphasis on European stockmarkets should assist in reversing the direction of flow. Naturally, any net flow from the US to Europe will assist the euro to regain its strength.

Central bank credibility

The ECB has had a tough time establishing its credibility, with both inflation and monetary growth stubbornly exceeding its targets. Of course, there are very significant differences in the performances of the individual euro economies and this casts doubt on the economic validity of the 'one size fits all' approach to interest rates. In contrast, the US Federal Reserve, is highly regarded. It will take many years – if ever – for the ECB to achieve equal status with the Fed.

Intervention to support the euro

The weakness of the euro led to several attempts in late 2000 to stabilize its value. The key events are shown in Figure 3-6. Given the fact that such little time has elapsed since the latest intervention, in November 2000, it is clearly impossible to draw any conclusions with regard to the long-term success of these attempts, although short-term results certainly appear favourable.

The euro: tracking its progress before 1999

The euro has only been in existence since 1 January 1999. However, for analytical and recording purposes, it is useful to construct a 'synthetic history' of the euro prior to that date. For example, if a company switched

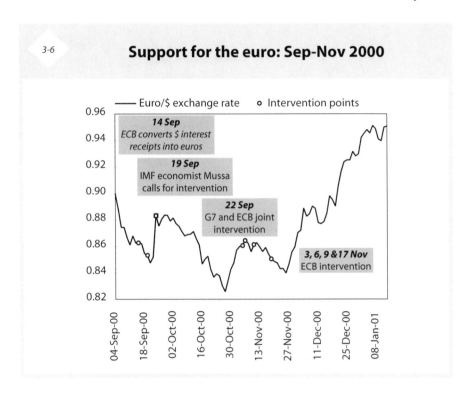

3-6

Support for the euro: Sep-Nov 2000

over to the euro in, say, 1999 and thus reported its accounts in euro from that date, there will be little in the way of comparative historical data – previous accounts would be denominated in the 'old' national currency. How can these historical accounts be updated to euro terms when the euro didn't exist at the time?

There are two main approaches to constructing a synthetic history. First, as one Ecu became one euro, the 'history' of the euro can be taken as the history of the Ecu. Using this method the history of the euro against the US dollar would, therefore, be the path of the Ecu against the dollar.

Second, the fixed conversion rates between the euro and national currencies can be used. For example, the conversion rate of $1=DM 1.95583 can be applied to the historic path of the Deutschemark against the dollar to create a euro history. An illustration of the two different methods is shown in Figure 3-7.

Generally, the paths of these two 'histories' are quite close , but significant divergence is displayed in the late 1970s and early 1980s. The reason for this is that, when the Ecu was launched in 1978, many of its constituent currencies were those of countries with high inflation rates. Since their exchange rates tended to depreciate over time, the net result was a weakening of the Ecu. This leads to a paradox: the (synthetic) euro

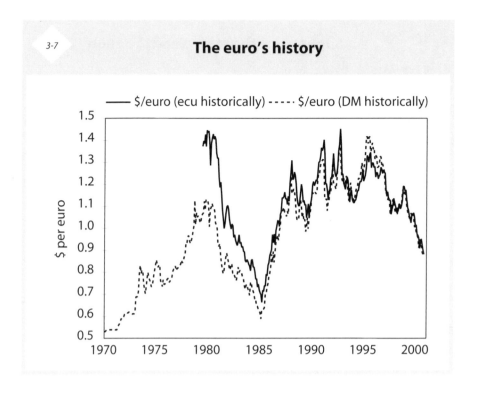

3-7   **The euro's history**

was much weaker in the 1980s on the basis of Ecu history than it was on the basis of Deutschemark history.

Conclusions

The creation of the euro through two separate channels – a one-for-one conversion from the Ecu; and the establishment of fixed conversion factors between the euro and its constituent currencies – was a complex process. The final stage of the euro's launch, with euro notes and coin replacing national currencies on 1 January 2002, means that the rather drawn out introduction of the euro is at last nearing its completion. The euro managed to confound many pundits by displaying an astonishing weakness during its first two years but, upon closer examination, certain attributing factors – notably concerning the US economy – can be identified. Since economic trends on both sides of the Atlantic appear to be changing, there are reasonable grounds for believing that the euro's weakness may now be coming to an end. However, even if the euro does attain a position of strength in a year or two, it will take much longer for the European Central bank to overcome its substantial credibility problems. Indeed, it may never happen.

4

What will the UK gain by joining the euro?

If, as seems likely, there is a referendum on the issue of the UK joining the euro, what will be the main arguments that are used in favour of the euro? This chapter seeks to identify the key benefits that are likely to be used to justify the UK joining the euro. It discusses primarily the economic, not the political, benefits. It includes some arguments in favour of joining which have a very sound basis. Others are more questionable, but are included as they have been a feature of the 'pro-euro' campaign so far. Where the benefits appear questionable, this is pointed out. The next chapter deals with the main disadvantages.

Advantage 1: exchange rate stability

Anyone who has travelled to, exported to, or imported from the eurozone countries over a number of years will undoubtedly have been affected by the substantial fluctuations in the value of sterling *vis-à-vis* the other national currencies. Comments such as "Remember how expensive it was in Spain when you got only 150 pesetas to the pound?" or "France is much cheaper now that you get more than ten francs to the pound again" have become common holiday conversation starters. Most people have a fair inkling of the sterling exchange rate against at least one European currency. Since the early 1990s, one pound has bought as few as 170 Spanish pesetas – when sterling was at its weakest in early 1993 – and as many as 280 pesetas in the summer of 2000. Against the franc, the story is similar: a rate as low as 7½ francs to the pound in 1995-1996, but then a strengthening of the pound to more than ten francs to the pound in late 1999. This took the rate against the franc back to levels last seen in the late 1980s.

If the UK joined the euro, such currency fluctuations would be eliminated. This exchange rate stability is the single most important

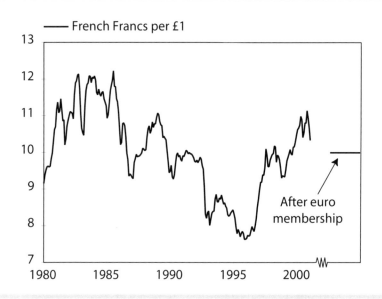

4-1

The ups and downs of sterling...

French Francs per £1

After euro membership

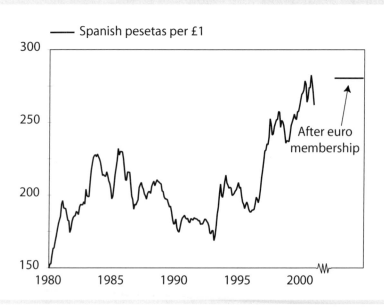

4-2

...would be a thing of the past

Spanish pesetas per £1

After euro membership

advantage of joining the euro. Most of the other benefits – and indeed, the disadvantages – stem from it.

All the twelve currencies that are members of the eurozone locked their exchange rates together as a prelude to introducing the euro itself (as described in Chapter 3) and, if the UK joined, its rate, too, would be locked. An illustration of the locked rates, assuming sterling enters at a rate of €1 = £0.798635, is given in Figure 4-3. (The reasons for this choice of exchange rate are revealed in Chapter 8).

Is it cheap or dear this year?

However, by the time the UK joins the euro, the twelve national currencies of the euro-area will, themselves, have been replaced by the euro. Saying that the UK will be locked to the French franc is, therefore, somewhat pointless if the French franc no longer exists as a legal tender currency.

In this sense the UK faces an 'easier' task in joining the euro than did the founding members. For the UK, only one conversion factor will actually be relevant (i.e. that against the euro) whereas the founders had to use a set of conversion factors against all other euro-area currencies for a period of three years.

Were the UK to join, there would be a period of, perhaps, two years, in which a fixed conversion factor would be in operation before sterling itself would be replaced by the euro. (Chapter 11 deals with the timetable in more detail.) Cash in circulation in the UK would only converted to euro at the end of that period.

4-3

The euro means fixed rates

The value of

**€1
equals:**

If sterling joined,

**£1 would
equal:***

1.95583	Deutschemarks		2.44479	Deutschemarks
40.3399	Belgian francs		50.5111	Belgian francs
40.3399	Luxembourg francs		50.5111	Luxembourg francs
2.20371	Dutch guilders		2.75935	Dutch guilders
1936.27	Italian lira		2424.47	Italian lira
166.386	Spanish pesetas		208.338	Spanish pesetas
200.482	Portuguese escudos		251.031	Portuguese escudos
6.55957	French francs		8.21348	French francs
0.787564	Irish punts		0.986138	Irish punts
13.7603	Austrian schillings		17.2298	Austrian schillings
5.94573	Finnish markka		7.44487	Finnish markka
340.750	Greek drachmas		426.665	Greek drachmas

*Assumes a conversion rate of €1 = £0.798635

Advantage 2: no costs of currency conversion

Naturally, if the UK shared the same currency with twelve other countries in Europe then there would be no need to change currencies. Hence there would no longer be any conversion costs which, aggregated for the entire economy, presently amount to between 0.5% and 1% of overall national output each year.

A practical example illustrates the effect of currency conversion costs more clearly. Prior to the launch of the euro, a tourist who started out in the UK with £100, and travelled to each of the fifteen EU countries, converting his money into each local currency as he entered the country would, in total, pay out around £50 on currency conversion costs alone.

Many large companies operating in the euro-area are already enjoying the advantage of the elimination of currency conversion costs. Large companies which have converted their treasury operations to function entirely in euros (something that has been possible since 1 January 1999, when the euro legally came into existence) claim quite large costs savings. Of course, those companies had to invest heavily in new IT, banking, treasury and accounting systems which enabled them to operate in euro. But, typically, companies claim the costs can be recouped quite quickly. Daimler Chrysler, for example, has said that the savings over two years will cover the costs of putting euro systems in place.

Small- and medium-sized companies in the euro-area have generally continued to operate in their national currencies, but, along with private individuals, they will see their currency conversion costs eliminated once euro notes and coin finally come into circulation on 1 January 2002.

Advantage 3: a more efficient single market

The single European market will operate more effectively once the euro is introduced. The combination of the single market (with free movement of goods, labour and capital) and a single currency will mean that many firms can operate more effectively on a pan-European basis, enjoying greater efficiencies and economies of scale. This advantage leads straight on to the next.

Advantage 4: transparency of prices and costs

Price transparency

If prices are expressed in one single currency across a wide area, then they are easier to compare or, to use financial terminology, there will be better 'price transparency'. Consumers should benefit as they will be able to shop around more effectively. No longer would there be a need to worry about the exchange rate underlying any price comparison. Rather, with all prices expressed in the same euro currency, it would simply no longer be an issue.

The scope for prices falling in response to such greater transparency is substantial. Many recent surveys show that there are still big price differences between different countries for the same item. For example, a recent survey by McKinsey was undertaken and its findings are reproduced in Figure 4-4.

The opportunity to take advantage of price transparency is likely to be greatest for high value, easily transportable items: cars are perhaps the prime example. Substantial price differentials between countries

---

4-4   **Price differentials**

Difference between highest and lowest prices

(Excluding tax, %)

Toothpaste*	180
Photo film*	120
Vehicle spare parts	50-100
Pharmaceuticals	50
CDs*	50
Industrial pumps	30-75
Cars	38
Construction equipment	30-40
Hi-fi systems *	25
Kitchen appliances	25
Newsprint	11
Tractors	10
Computers	10

Prices charged by manufacturers to distributors except *=consumer prices

Source: McKinsey

continue to exist in this area, with the UK almost invariably the most expensive market.

It would be most unrealistic to expect prices to be *the same* everywhere. Regional differences in prices exist in the UK and even bigger regional differences should be expected within the euro-area itself. In particular:

- there are differences in tax rates between different euro-area countries;

- there are different specifications in different markets (for example, the UK has right-hand drive cars and 3-pin electrical plugs!)

- there are costs involved in shopping around (e.g. postage and packing) which may be disproportionate for small-value items.

Furthermore, other changes in the economy may be just as important in introducing price competition. For example, the greater use of the internet and the larger role played by US-style discount stores are significant factors.

On balance, there would clearly be a benefit from price transparency for consumers, but its extent is rather difficult to quantify.

Cost transparency

Consumers are not the only ones to benefit. Costs would also be expressed in a common currency and 'cost transparency' means that suppliers would find it easier to compare the costs of their supplies from different sources.

Take the example of buyer for a UK food retailer. Suppose he buys tomatoes and can obtain these from Spain, Italy, France or Portugal. He has to plan ahead for the next season and so is concerned about changes in the exchange rate, because he will have to pay his supplier some months in the future when exchange rates may have changed. Prior to the launch of the euro he was concerned about fluctuations in the value of the peseta, the lira, the franc and the escudo against sterling. With all four currencies now fixed in value to the euro, his job is much simpler, as his four potential suppliers all set their selling prices in euro. His sole concern is the sterling-euro exchange rate.

If the UK joined the euro his job would be even simpler. Not only would all his costs be in euro; his selling prices in the UK would also be in euro.

In other industries the benefits of cost transparency, combined with the savings on currency conversion costs, can be substantial. The tourism industry, for example, has stated that, although it will face one-off costs of around 1.5% of turnover in order to prepare for the euro, the cost savings

4-5

European tourism

Costs:
1.5% of turnover, one-off

Savings:
3.0% of turnover, continuing each year

– an aggregate of cost transparency and currency conversion savings – will amount to around 3% of turnover per year.

Price transparency versus cost transparency
...and the impact on profits

Some companies may be able to take advantage of cost transparency and reduce their costs before they face the pressures from consumers seeking greater price transparency. Their profit margins might therefore improve as a result of the UK joining the euro. To use the food retailing example again, it would seem rather unlikely that euro-area consumers will shop around in different countries for the best price for fresh tomatoes. The food retailer may, as we described, be able to realize the benefit of cost transparency without 'giving it away' as a result of greater price transparency.

In other industries, however, the opposite is clearly the case. Many companies already have managed to cut costs in response to competitive pressures, and so the benefits of 'cost transparency' may not be that significant. They would, however, come under increased consumer pressure for lower prices as a result of price transparency. Electrical goods retailers are generally considered to be in this category.

In overall terms, the McKinsey study cited above concluded that manufacturers' selling prices would be cut, on average, by 2 to 3% as a result of price transparency, and that profit margins could fall by between 15% and 50%.

Advantage 5: lower interest rates

Wim Duisenberg, the president of the European Central bank, when taking a taxi from Heathrow airport to central London, was asked by the taxi driver "How will I benefit if the UK joins the euro?" Duisenberg replied that his mortgage rate would be lower and that there was a simple choice – join the euro and get low interest rates; or keep sterling and have higher rates.

When the comment was made, in late 1999, UK interest rates were almost twice the eurozone level. Even though the gap has subsequently narrowed, UK rates still remain above those of its euro neighbours.

If the UK joined the euro, then it would have the same level of interest rates as all of the other members of the euro-area. To be more precise, a common interest rate for all of the members of the euro-area would be set, as it is now, by the European Central Bank. It would then be implemented and made effective by the Bank of England, who would thus be acting essentially as an operating division of the ECB, and would have no authority to set rates above or below the common euro interest rate .

A detailed description of the way in which the Bank of England and the ECB currently set interest rates, and the ways in which this would change, are described in Chapter 10.

Can we be sure that interest rates will be lower?

We need to consider this perceived advantage rather carefully. Although, as this book is written early in 2001, euro-area interest rates are lower than those in the UK, it is by no means certain that this will remain the case.

First, there is a caveat, along the lines of 'past performance is not a guide to the future', which normally appears alongside investment recommendations. In the case of the ECB, this caveat is equally appropriate, indeed perhaps more so. The ECB has only been setting euro-area interest rates for just over two years, so its past performance is certainly very limited.

Second, if we look back at the years prior to 1999, we can formulate a synthetic euro interest rate – in much the same way as the synthetic euro exchange rate discussed in Chapter 3 – on the basis of either Ecu interest rates or Deutschemark interest rates (or, indeed, the trend in interest rates of any of the euro-area countries). This shows that, in recent years, UK interest rates have only quite rarely slipped below euro interest rates. However, after sterling was forced out of the ERM in 1992, UK interest

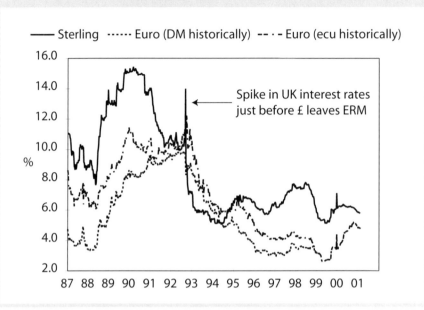

4-6

Sterling and euro interest rates

—— Sterling   ⋯⋯ Euro (DM historically)   –– · – Euro (ecu historically)

Spike in UK interest rates just before £ leaves ERM

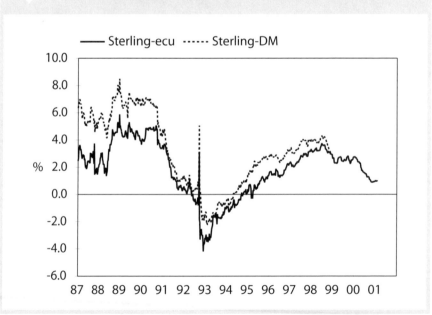

4-7

Sterling-euro interest rate differential

—— Sterling-ecu   ⋯⋯ Sterling-DM

rates were cut to below German levels and stayed below for some eighteen months (and remained below Ecu interest rates for two years, see Figures 4-6 and 4-7). Clearly, this would not be possible if the UK joined the euro. In Chapter 5, we consider whether this is a disadvantage.

What about mortgage rates?

The common euro interest rate across all countries in the eurozone refers only to the official rate set by the ECB. Commercial banks, mortgage providers, credit card companies and so on are, of course, free to set their own interest rates. These bear a relationship to the central bank's official interest rate, but often quite a loose one.

For example, in the UK mortgage market there is intense competition, with companies offering diverse inducements to borrowers, such as fixed rates, discounts, caps, cash back offers and so on. This diversity would not be reduced as a result of the UK joining the euro – indeed, it may well be increased. In the euro-area, a much larger proportion of mortgages are at fixed rates than in the UK (although the UK proportion has risen in recent times). It may be that euro-area banks, who have greater expertise in offering fixed rate mortgages, would bring a new level of competitiveness to the market, thus forcing UK mortgage providers to enhance the range of mortgage products available.

This diversity in the mortgage market, coupled with the relatively loose relationship between official interest rates and mortgage rates, means that Mr Duisenberg's assertion that the taxi driver had a choice of a lower mortgage if the UK joined the euro, or a higher mortgage if the UK did not join, is not beyond dispute.

Advantage 6: higher house prices?

Some have claimed that there could be a rise in house prices as a result of the UK joining the euro. Several factors are at work:

- *interest rates will be lower.*
  As discussed above, however, the change may not be that great and indeed there is no way of being sure that UK rates would be lower than they would have been if the UK had not joined the euro.

- *more widespread use of cheaper fixed rates.*
  Greater availability of fixed rate mortgages may be a result of the UK joining the euro, but long-term interest rates are actually lower in the UK than in the euro area at the moment. It is likely, however, that if the UK did join, long-term rates would be very similar to the rates in other euro-area countries

- *The UK will be a more attractive base for European companies.*
  Certainly, there has been concern recently that, if the UK stayed out
  of the euro, companies might prefer to locate in the euro-area. The
  issue is difficult to quantify, but is examined in more detail in
  Chapter 6 (as the effect on inward investment and jobs are two of
  Gordon Brown's five tests on whether the UK should join the euro).

Of course, higher house prices are only an advantage for those already
owning a house. Furthermore, there may be differences in regional house
price movements if the UK joined the euro-area. On balance, it is difficult
to claim any very substantial advantage from possible developments in
the housing market.

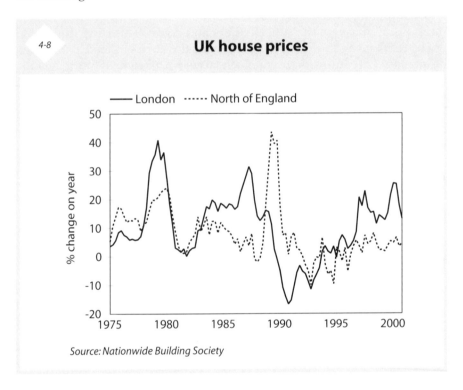

4-8

UK house prices

Source: Nationwide Building Society

Advantage 7: Improvements in financial markets

The potential improvements in the mortgage market would be just part
of an overall potential improvement in the UK's financial markets if the
UK joins the euro. Since they were launched in 1999, the euro financial
markets have grown rapidly, both in their size and in the range of
products that are available. This means that many euro-area companies

have better access to financial markets, and on more competitive terms, than they did in their previous domestic markets. For example, a Portuguese company (which may have found it quite difficult and expensive to obtain finance from the escudo capital markets before 1999) now has the ability to tap into the euro markets, where a wider range of financial products is on offer.

These benefits are probably greater for larger companies than they are for small- and medium-sized companies. UK large companies can, of course, raise finance in the euro capital markets even if the UK stays 'out'. It is doubtful, however, that the full benefits can accessed unless the UK joins.

Conclusions

There are undoubtedly key advantages to the UK joining the euro. Initially, the most obvious saving may be in currency conversion costs. Furthermore, the potential benefits from price transparency may also be substantial. On the other had, although interest rates may be lower if the UK joins the euro, this benefit is far from certain. Indeed, it is in the area of interest rate determination that most of the potential disadvantages lie. We turn to these in the next chapter.

5

The disadvantages of joining the euro

In the last chapter, we looked at the perceived advantages of the UK joining the euro. In this chapter, we turn the tables and take a look at the downside. We look particularly at the recent problems faced by Ireland, an economy which has many similar characteristics to the UK.

Disadvantage 1: the 'one-size-fits-all' approach to interest rates

We have already noted that the ECB sets the short-term interest rate for all euro-area countries. Clearly, any rate thus set by the ECB is unlikely to suit all countries – some may find it too high, others too low.

A good example of the shortcomings of this one-size-fits-all approach can be found in Ireland, a founder member of the euro. Since joining the euro, Ireland has had:

- very strong economic growth (averaging three times the rate of other euro-area countries);

- a high inflation rate (in the year 2000, this reached 7% – which was significantly above the ECB's target of 2% for the euro-area as a whole); and

- there has been a boom in the property market.

There is little doubt that, had a rate been set purely on the basis of Ireland's domestic needs, it would have been higher, perhaps significantly so. This problem was predictable – and was foreseen by many economists before Ireland joined the euro-area. The issue now is whether other measures can be use to deal with the problem. We take a look at these under 'Disadvantage 3'.

Similar problems can reasonably be expected if the UK joins the euro. There is a parallel with the experience of the UK in the Exchange Rate Mechanism (ERM) in 1990-1992. The desire to reduce interest rates in the UK because the economy remained weak was frustrated by the fact that Germany, at the time, was maintaining high interest rates in order to curb the inflationary effects of German reunification. As Germany set the low-point for interest rates in the ERM, and since sterling was at the weakest extreme permitted in the ERM, there was no scope for a reduction in UK rates. Indeed, there were calls for yet higher rates in order to support sterling's value. This conflict between what was needed to underpin the currency (higher interest rates) and what was needed to help the domestic economy (lower interest rates) directly led to the UK being forced out of the ERM.

As soon as Britain left the mechanism, UK interest rates were cut aggressively, to a level which was below those prevailing in Germany. Norman Lamont, the chancellor of the exchequer at the time, was reported to be 'singing in his bath' at the possibility of setting 'British interest rates on the basis of what was needed for the British economy'.

The ability to deal with economic shocks – such as German reunification – is one of Gordon Brown's tests for the suitability of the UK joining the euro (see Chapter 6). The main issue is that, if the UK joins the euro, there will be no scope to adjust UK interest rates in response to specific UK circumstances. Other ways of making adjustments to the economy will, therefore, have to be found.

Disadvantage 2: no chance to devalue

The 'other way', which has often been employed in the UK, is to allow sterling's value to fall against other currencies. Indeed, after sterling was forced out of the ERM in 1992, sterling fell in value substantially against other European currencies. This made UK exports cheaper and, coupled with lower interest rates, provided a 'double boost' for the economy. If the UK joined the euro, the possibility for a devaluation against the other countries of the euro-area would obviously disappear, since there would be no exchange rate to change. Furthermore, it would be impossible to 'engineer' any devaluation against other currencies, such as the US dollar. Indeed, the relative value of the dollar to the UK economy could only vary as a result of changes in the overall value of the euro, over which the UK would have little direct control.

Disadvantage 3: taxes might have to rise

If interest rates cannot be adjusted to meet the needs of the domestic economy, and devaluation is out of the question, the one remaining option available to the government is adjustment of fiscal policy. In essence, this means raising taxes and cutting government spending if the economy is growing too strongly; or cutting taxes and raising government spending when the economy is in need of boost. However, these Keynesian policies have been widely discredited in recent years as they have tended to be misused, leading to an ever-increasing share of government in the economy. Furthermore, the timing of tax and spending changes is often poorly judged, and any 'benefits' for the economy normally manifest themselves only after an uncertain, but often lengthy, time lag. Thus any resultant boost may actually arrive when the economy is starting to recover under its own steam (and vice versa).

Returning to the current example of Ireland, some way of reining in the growth of the economy, and dampening inflation, is clearly needed. As we have noted, with no ability to change its interest rate, a fiscal policy change is the only available remedy – meaning that taxes need to be increased and/or government spending cut. In fact, Ireland is under considerable pressure from the European Commission to instigate precisely these fiscal measures.

Ireland, however, is conducting a fiscal policy that is – by the standards set out for running the single currency – exemplary. It has a substantial budget surplus, expected to be near to 7% of the economy in 2001, while its stock of government debt is being repaid very quickly and is already well below the 60% of GDP threshold set in the Maastricht Treaty (see Figure 5-1 & 5-2). In these circumstances, the notion of a tighter fiscal policy – entailing an even bigger budget surplus and an even more rapid repayment of government debt – is not one which the Irish government views favourably. How, indeed, can the case be made for increasing taxes further when the economy already has a big budget surplus? The parallel with George W. Bush's policies is that politicians, in these circumstances, want to "give the money back", not ask for more.

In any case, there are restrictions on the extent to which taxes can be increased in order to manage the economy. Greater price transparency resulting from the use of the euro means that the ability to set tax rates that are substantially out of line with other euro-area countries is very much reduced. The UK already faces pressures to reduce taxation levels on alcohol and tobacco because they are higher than in other EU countries, and these pressures would become significantly greater if the UK were to join the eurozone. Similarly, many companies may relocate their operations if corporate taxation in one country is seen as excessive.

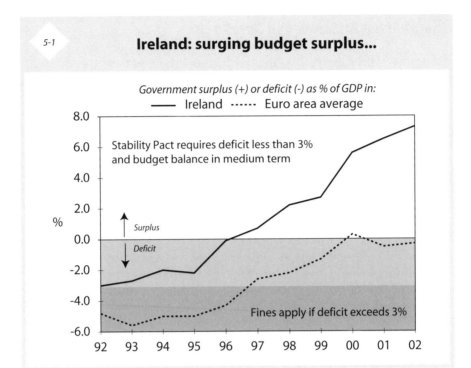

5-1

Ireland: surging budget surplus...

Government surplus (+) or deficit (-) as % of GDP in:
—— Ireland ······ Euro area average

Stability Pact requires deficit less than 3% and budget balance in medium term

Surplus

Deficit

Fines apply if deficit exceeds 3%

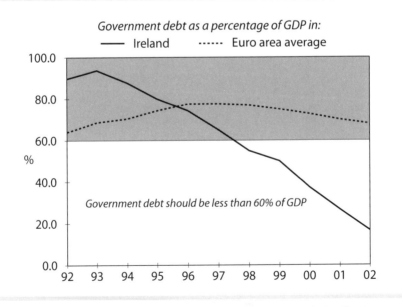

5-2

...and declining debt stock

Government debt as a percentage of GDP in:
—— Ireland ······ Euro area average

Government debt should be less than 60% of GDP

Furthermore, there may also be some limit on the extent to which personal taxation can differ between countries.

Disdavantage 4: overall lack of control over the economy

If the UK joins the euro:

- it would lose the power to set national interest rates – the common level of euro rates would be imposed on the UK;

- there would be no exchange rate against other countries in the euro-area, thus there would be no way of devaluing or revaluing against these currencies;

- there would be no direct control over the rate between the euro and other currencies, such as the US dollar;

- the UK may face pressures to implement fiscal changes in government taxation and/or spending in order to manage the economy, but these may unfeasible, both economically and/or politically.

It is the aggregate effect of these changes, which together effectively remove domestic control over the UK economy, that causes the greatest concern.

Disadvantage 5: costs involved in the changeover

The costs involved in any changeover to the euro are likely to be substantial (see Figure 5-3). Moreover these costs are largely 'up front', being paid in the preparation period. The advantages would generally come later, particularly once companies and consumers have switched over fully to operating in euros and have become familiar with the new currency.

Some of the main costs for companies stem from:

- The preparation for, and management, of the changeover.
  Typically a company would need a 'euro task force' to prepare and manage the changeover, co-ordinating the work carried out in different departments. Various checklists of tasks have been produced by organizations such as the Federation of European Accountants (see their website www.euro.fee.be)

- Dual pricing in both sterling and euros.
  The length of time this is done, and its extent, would vary from company to company. Generally companies selling high-value items with a low

turnover would incur the lowest costs; conversely, those with lower value items with a high turnover would incur the highest costs.

- Staff training on the new currency.

- Handling of two currencies for the period when they circulate side-by-side.
  This would be a greater burden for companies which handle large amounts of cash, such as the small retail sector.

- Installation of new systems which are capable of operating in euro

- Changeover of coin-operated equipment such as vending machines, ticket machines, supermarket trolleys, etc.

- Dealing with customer enquiries about the changeover to the euro.

The retail sector would face, proportionately, the largest costs, and these are explored in more detail in Chapter 12. In aggregate, they may amount to around 2% of turnover (see Figure 5-3). Similar costs are reported by the banks and the tourism industry. AMUE (the Association for the Monetary Union for Europe) reports a rather lower estimate of costs.

5-3   ## Costs of changing from sterling to the euro

Coverage:	Source:	Basis:
Banks	European Banking Union	2% of costs for two years
EU tourism industry	Own estimates	1.5% turnover
Retail sector	Eurocommerce	1.8%-2.5% of turnover
All businesses	AMUE	0.1%-0.5% of turnover

The range of estimates partly reflects the fact that it is often difficult to differentiate the costs due to the euro changeover from those which would have occurred anyway. A new computer system or a new piece of software, which may be purchased whether the UK enters the euro or not, could help a company prepare for the euro. Similarly, any new technology that is put in place to help with the changeover to the euro may have additional benefits.

Disadvantage 6: relative prices may change

The process of converting from sterling to euro may involve the rounding up of some prices and the rounding down of others (see Chapter 12 for an example of why this might be the case). The result would be a change in relative prices of different goods.

Disadvantage 7: general confusion

There is a risk that general confusion would surround the changeover process. Decimalization in the UK was an exercise which required many years of preparation and planning. That change involved only the 'subsidiary units' of sterling, i.e. shillings and pence. The changeover to the euro goes further, in that sterling itself would be changed. Moreover, the conversion factor between sterling and the euro, would likely be a quite inconvenient number, expressed to six significant figures, for example:

$$€1 = £0.798635$$

It would be legally binding to use the conversion rate. No shortening or rounding of the conversion rate would be allowed. For example, it would not be permissible to use:

$$€1 = 80 \text{ pence}$$

This conversion rate would be used for a transition period before the full adoption of the euro took place and also, after that, for converting any sterling contracts into euro terms. Calculators programmed with the conversion factor would be widely available and this should help the process, but even so, many may find it hard to adjust.

Conclusions

The main disadvantage of joining the euro relates to the loss of control over the domestic economy. Whether this is framed in terms of the loss of control over economic policy or, more simply, in terms of a loss of sovereignty is almost immaterial.

The other economic disadvantage involves the costs associated with the changeover to the euro. These can be viewed as one-off charges, since they would not recur once the UK had joined. Nevertheless, they could be substantial, especially for the retail sector.

6

Does the euro pass Gordon Brown's tests?

In October 1997, shortly after the Labour party came to office, the chancellor of the exchequer, Gordon Brown, set out five 'tests' which would be used to judge whether it would be in the interest of the UK to join the euro. These are:

- whether the UK economy has achieved sustainable convergence with the economies of the euro-area;
- whether there would be sufficient flexibility to respond to shocks if the UK joined the euro-area;
- the impact on investment in the UK;
- the impact on the UK financial services industry;
- and the impact on employment.

If, as is expected, the Labour party is re-elected in 2001 for another term of office, Tony Blair has said that the Treasury will assess whether the UK passes these tests within the first two years of the next parliament. If the Treasury judges that the tests are passed, membership of the euro would then be recommended by the government, there would be a vote in parliament and the issue would be put to a referendum. The timetable for joining the euro is discussed in more detail in Chapter 11. Here, we deal with the issues surrounding Mr Brown's tests.

Convergence

The first test is whether there is 'sustainable convergence' between the UK and the economies of the eurozone. Convergence in this sense means that the UK economy and the eurozone economies are growing at a similar rate and are at a similar stage of their economic cycle. This is

6-1   # Gordon Brown's tests

The tests of whether it would be suitable for the UK to join the euro are:

1 whether there is sustainable convergence between the UK and the economies of the eurozone

2 whether there would be sufficient flexibility in the UK economy to respond to shocks if it joined the eurozone

3 the effect of the euro on investment in the UK

4 the effect of the euro on the UK financial services industry

5 the effect of the euro on UK employment

arguably the most important of the five tests. Suppose, for example, the UK economy was growing strongly and inflationary pressures were starting to develop. In the past, the first signs of inflationary pressure in the UK have often manifested themselves in, for example, a strong housing market, a sharp rise in equity prices, and labour market shortages which put upward pressure on wage increases. Such pressures normally encourage the Bank of England to raise interest rates in order to dampen any inflationary tendencies . For example, the Bank responded in just such a way when inflationary signals began to emerge in late 1999 and early 2000. However, if, at the same time that the UK was in that situation, eurozone countries were experiencing quite contrasting conditions – say, weaker growth and little inflationary pressure, then there would be no calls for a similar rise in interest rates in that area. Thus, if the UK were a member of the eurozone, there would clearly be difficulty in setting an interest rate that was suitable both for the strong economic growth conditions in the UK and the not-so-strong conditions of the eurozone.

These problems would be mitigated – although probably not avoided altogether – if the UK's economic growth was closely aligned to that of the eurozone countries. This is the reason behind Mr Brown's test. Moreover, to feel truly comfortable that problems were not likely to arise in the future, this condition should be met in an ongoing manner, for a reasonably long period of time – several years, if not decades.

The data, however, do not support the view that there is a strong correlation between overall GDP growth in the UK and that in the eurozone. Taking a long period – the forty years spanning the 1960s, 1970s, 1980s and 1990s – the average correlation between growth in the UK and the eurozone is negative. What this means is that, typically, when the UK economy is growing, the eurozone economy is contracting. However, this overall picture of the forty years masks the fact the lack of correlation between the UK and the eurozone was concentrated mainly in the 1990s. In the previous thirty years, the correlation had been positive – albeit not particularly strong.

In contrast, over the entire forty year period, the correlation of UK with the US economy was much stronger than that with the eurozone. Indeed, during the 1990s, this correlation with the US became even more marked. On the basis of such evidence, the UK would be better placed to form a monetary union with the US than with the eurozone.

6-2

The UK: closer to the US than the eurozone

Correlation coefficients, %	UK & USA	UK & Eurozone
1960s	0	23
1970s	54	67
1980s	42	65
1990s	79	-46
1960-1999	69	-23
2000 (est.)	35	-13

Note: Correlation coefficient of 100% indicates perfect positive correlation between growth rates, e.g. if the US grows by 4% and the UK by 4%.

Correlation coefficient of minus 100% indicates perfect negative correlation between growth rates, e.g. if the US grows by 4% and the UK economy contracts by 4%.

Correlation coefficient of zero indicates no correlation.

Another way of assessing the relationship with the eurozone is to look at the correlation between the UK and individual countries within the eurozone. Such a study was carried out by the IMF for the period 1964 to 1990 and is updated here. The IMF viewed Germany as the 'anchor country' for Europe and looked at correlations of growth between different European countries and Germany. The closest correlations were with Germany's near neighbours and closest trading partners – the Netherlands, France, Austria and Belgium. The UK had the weakest correlation – just 19% (100% is a perfect positive correlation, 0% is no correlation and minus 100% is a perfect negative correlation).

In the subsequent ten years, the correlation became negative. This meant that, rather than being loosely correlated with German growth, the UK economy typically headed in the opposite direction: if the UK was booming, Germany was in recession and vice versa.

6-3	**Not anchored?**			
		1964-1990		**1991-1999**
Correlation coefficients of growth with Germany, the 'anchor' area of the EU (%)	Germany	100		100
	Greece	61		61
	Austria	70		56
	Belgium	71		23
	Portugal	49		22
	Italy	47		19
	Spain	54		19
	Netherlands	77		7
	France	71		6
	Denmark	61		-6
	Sweden	43		-17
	Ireland	48		-37
	Finland	41		-55
	UK	19		-64

The broad conclusion of the data presented here is that there is no close convergence between the growth rates of the UK and the eurozone. The UK Treasury's study, when it is produced, will be a more comprehensive study than that of the IMF. It will presumably consider different measures of economic growth (either overall GDP growth, as we use here, or just growth in the domestic economy) and a variety of time periods. It seems highly unlikely, however, that the study can conclude that there is close convergence between the UK and eurozone economies, unless it is highly selective about the time periods used and the choice of data.

Gordon Brown's Tests.

Ability to cope with economic shocks

The ability to cope with economic shocks is related to the convergence requirement. The term 'shock' is used in this context to describe various external or unexpected factors that affect economies. Examples include a sharp change in the oil price, a sudden weakening of the euro against the dollar or a technological change (such as the development of the internet). The ability to cope with shocks depends on two factors.

In the first place, there is a need to examine whether the eurozone economies and the UK respond in a similar way to a given shock. Second, if they do not correspond, whether there are various mechanisms – either automatic or specifically designed as part of government policy – which are capable of offsetting the effect.

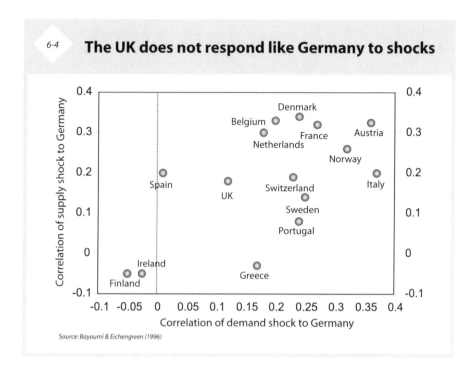

6-4   **The UK does not respond like Germany to shocks**

Source: Bayoumi & Eichengreen (1996)

Two studies have shown that the UK has not, in the past, responded to shocks in a similar manner to eurozone economies. Again, it was found that a 'core' group of European countries (Belgium, the Netherlands, France and Austria) responded in a similar way to Germany (regarded as the anchor area). The correlation of the UK's reaction to the shocks and the reaction of Germany was, however, close to zero. Factors explaining this include the fact that the UK is less susceptible to oil shocks (as it is a net oil exporter, whereas eurozone economies are not) and differences in the structure of the economies and the financial systems.

If there were methods of offsetting the different responses to shocks, then the variance in such responses would arguably be less important. However, with a common interest rate among the euro-area countries, there is no chance of altering rates to offset the responses. Equally, the common use of the euro rules out any changes to a country's exchange rate. As a result, there are just two main ways in which adjustment can take place in the euro-area: through government fiscal policy and/or through labour migration.

In the US, for example, where different states respond in different ways to shocks, government fiscal policy can offset some of the different effects. If the oil producing states are booming in response to a high oil price, say, but the Midwest is suffering because of a weakness in the auto industry, federal transfers can ease the differences. Higher taxation in Texas can help pay for a bigger social security bill in Detroit. There is limited scope for this to happen within the eurozone, as most fiscal policy decisions are taken by national governments not by a central authority. There is only a limited 'central' EU budget which, in any case, is used primarily for longer-term structural purposes, not to smooth out shorter-term economic fluctuations.

The other solution to shocks affecting different areas differently is for labour to move. Again, this happens in the US but does not work as effectively in the eurozone. In any one year, some 3% of the US population moves from one state to another. In Europe, however, only around 1% will move from one region of a particular country to another region of that *same* country. Labour mobility is simply not as high as in the US, although there are two professions of which this cannot be said: football players and investment bankers. Needless to say, that is unlikely to be a strong enough basis on which to support UK membership of the eurozone!

The conclusion is that it seems very unlikely that the Treasury will be able to judge, credibly, that this test is met.

6-5

Labour mobility

Regional moves as % total population*

Italy	0.5
England & Wales	1.1
Germany	1.1
France	1.3
USA	2.8

* the proportion of the population moving from one region of the country to another region of the same country

Source: Oxford Economic Forecasting

The euro and investment

Over the course of 1999 and 2000, there were several pronouncements by manufacturing companies to the effect that investment in the UK would be impeded as a result of the UK staying out of the euro-area. Nevertheless, in a highly-publicized move, the Japanese car giant Nissan elected to build its new Micra car in Sunderland, even though the company had indicated concern about the level of sterling and sought clarification of the UK government's future policy on the euro. It seems unlikely that Nissan obtained any such assurance – if for no other reason than no-one can predict the outcome of the promised referendum on UK entry.

Any attempt to quantify the effects on investment of a decision to join, or not to join, the euro is fraught with difficulties. In reality, decisions whether or not to invest in the UK are based on a wide range of considerations, including:

- the productivity of workers in the UK;
- the skills possessed by UK workers (technical skills, language skills etc.);
- the quality of the transport system and general infrastructure;
- the overall flexibility of working practices;
- the nature and stability of the government;
- taxation levels;
- the extent of subsidies.

Isolating the impact of the euro from all the other factors is extremely difficult and it remains to be seen what approach the UK Treasury will use in order to try to achieve this.

Of course, the issue surrounding the euro itself is also often confused. For example, are companies primarily concerned about the actuality of the UK joining the euro? Or are they rather more concerned about the strength of sterling against the euro, which makes UK labour costs higher in relation to the rest of Europe, and export prices relatively lower? Perhaps they have a problem with sterling's volatility, which makes future planning more difficult. Again, identifying the influence of each of these aspects of exchange rate uncertainty is difficult.

Given this, it seems that it will be difficult for the Treasury to present a convincing case – either way – on the impact of investment.

The impact on the City

Similar considerations apply to the issue of whether the City of London would suffer from the UK being outside the euro-area. Once again, there are a wide variety of factors at work when firms determine whether or not to locate in London. So far, the fact that the UK has remained outside the euro-area has not been a major impediment to the City. London remains the leading European – and indeed global – financial centre for a wide variety of activities. For example, the Bank of England's publication, *Practical Issues Arising from the Euro* (November 2000), cites the following information in support of London's role as an international financial centre:

- 32% of global foreign exchange turnover takes place in London, compared with 18% in New York, London's nearest rival. In Europe, Germany accounts for just 5% and France 4%;

- there are more than 450 foreign banking institutions in London, almost twice the number of Frankfurt, London's nearest European rival;

- turnover on the London International Financial Futures Exchange (LIFFE) is almost double that on EUREX, its closest European rival;

- more than half of euro-denominated eurobond issuance has consistently taken place in London since the euro was launched

The longer-term issue, of course, is whether London can maintain this strong position if the UK were to stay out of the euro.

The euro and employment

The impact on employment is related both to the effect on investment and to the impact on the City. Given that there seems, as yet, no convincing evidence of a substantial negative effect from being outside the euro, it is hard to claim that the impact on jobs is likely to be particularly great. The unemployment rate in the UK also continues to be well below that in the euro-area (see Figure 6-6).

Conclusions

The Treasury's assessment of Mr Brown's tests will clearly be more comprehensive and detailed than the one presented here. However, it seems unlikely that any really convincing case can be built stating that the UK passes the tests could be seen as assertion, not judgement.

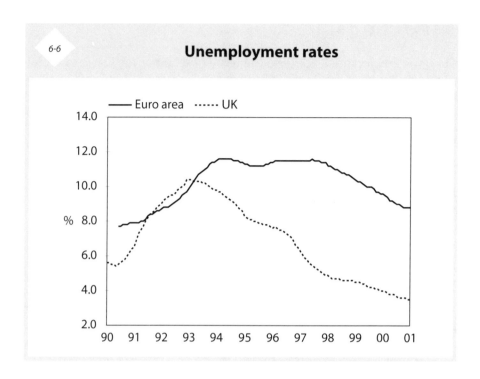

6-6

Unemployment rates

Indeed, the fact that the UK clearly fails the first two tests – on economic convergence and the ability to deal with shocks – seems, at this stage, to be an almost insurmountable obstacle to the UK joining the euro.

7

Does the UK pass the EU's tests?

In the last chapter, we looked at whether the UK would pass Gordon Brown's tests. In essence, the application of these tests is to ensure that the UK would gain benefit from membership of the euro club. However, wanting to join a club is one thing, gaining admittance is quite another and the EU, like most clubs, has its own criteria to ensure that undesirables are kept out. These criteria were first set down in 1992 at the Treaty of Maastricht, and thus they are unsurprisingly labelled the 'Maastricht Criteria'. So, the UK may knock at the door of the club, but it is up to the doorman to let us in and, in the EU's case, there are two of them – the European Commission and the European Central Bank. These two will each produce a report, based on the Maastricht criteria, assessing whether the UK is suitable to be admitted.

However, even if the reports by these 'doormen' do recommend that the UK should be admitted, that does not signify direct and immediate entry. Their recommendations must go before the European Council (comprising the heads of state of all the EU member states) for formal approval.

At a recent press conference, Wim Duisenberg, the president of the European Central bank, made the importance of these tests clear. referring to Mr Brown's tests, he said:

*"It is **only** the Maastricht criteria which I regard as relevant for eventual entry of the UK into monetary union. When the time is ripe it will be on those criteria that the ECB will write a conversion report."*

What exactly are these criteria? There are five in all:

- The UK government's budget deficit
- The UK's outstanding stock of government debt
- The UK's inflation rate
- The UK's bond yield
- The sterling exchange rate

The EU's tests.

We shall now consider the first four criteria (none of which should prove too troublesome for the UK). In the case of each test, we shall consider:

- why the test is applied;
- whether the UK would pass the test on current form;
- whether the UK is likely to pass the test in the future; and
- how well the UK performs in relation to other euro-area countries.

Government's budget deficit

The first of the Maastricht criteria is that a government's budget deficit should be no more than 3% of GDP.

The main reason for this restriction is that large deficits tend to stimulate an economy, causing demand to rise and thus threatening to push up inflation. To suppress inflation, or merely the threat of inflation, interest rates are often raised. It would clearly be problematical for the European Central Bank if any country within the euro club suffered a large deficit, since interest rates must stay the same throughout the euro-area (the so-called 'one size fits all' feature). Thus, from the EU's point of view, the last person they want in their club is someone possessing a large deficit. Some deficit (3% of GDP) is, however, permissible.

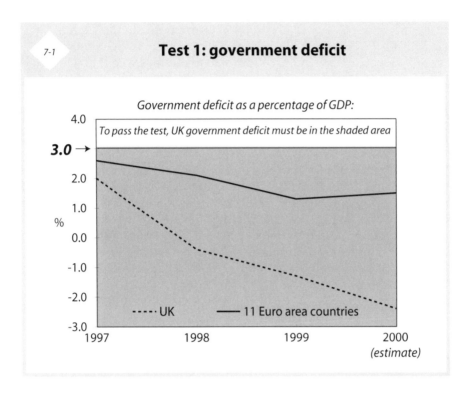

7-1

Test 1: government deficit

Government deficit as a percentage of GDP:

To pass the test, UK government deficit must be in the shaded area

---- UK   —— 11 Euro area countries

1997   1998   1999   2000
(estimate)

Looking at the figures for 1999 and 2000, it is clear that the UK comfortably passes the test. Indeed, in both years, and in 1998 as well, the UK actually managed to run a budget surplus! In contrast, euro-area countries managed to record an average deficit of 1.5% of GDP in 2000. Back in March 1998, when decisions were being made about the initial tranche of euro countries, many states found the deficit requirement to be a major problem. Indeed, in the case of France and Italy, much financial engineering was needed in a last-minute attempt to come within the 3% limit. Special taxes, adjustments to state pension entitlements and an acceleration in the privatization of state assets all featured in this desperate, though ultimately successful, attempt.

The UK's current position, however, stands in sharp contrast. There is no need to massage the data as, on a straightforward basis, the UK easily passes the test. However, notwithstanding the current healthy position, an element of caution would not go amiss. There is a chance, albeit a slim one, that a sharp slowdown in the UK economy in the coming years would push the UK government's budget back into deficit again. That said, the chances of even coming close to the 3% limit are small.

Of course, at this point, one could be forgiven for thinking that the 3% test is merely a way of sorting out the undesirables at the door of the club and that, once in, it wouldn't matter what happened. Not so. The club has its own 'house rules', and one of them is embodied in the 'Stability and Growth Pact'. There is a permanent ceiling on the budget deficit at the same 3% level for all member countries. If a country exceeds that level it is 'fined', with the severity of the fine increasing depending on how large the deficit is and how long it remains uncorrected.

The outstanding stock of the government's debt

The second test calls for the outstanding stock of government debt to be below 60% of GDP. Basically, government debt reflects the amount of debt that a state has chalked up over the years and so this requirement mainly ensures that no one entering the club has such a large amount of debt as to bring the club's membership into disrepute. All states like to have their own good credit rating and the fear is that if one looks shaky, they will all be viewed in a similar light, thus causing problems for the club as a whole.

Most of the outstanding government debt of the euro-area member countries was changed from their individual national currencies into euros at the start of 1999, while all new government bonds issued since then have been denominated in euros. This does not mean, however, that

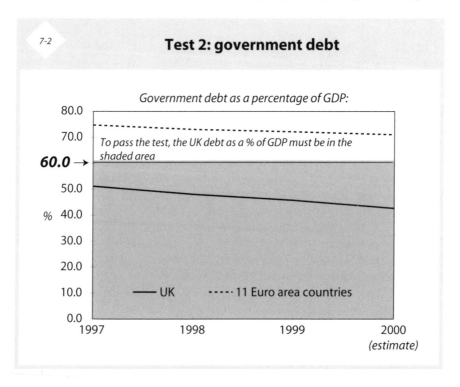

7-2

Test 2: government debt

Government debt as a percentage of GDP:

To pass the test, the UK debt as a % of GDP must be in the shaded area

——— UK   ·····11 Euro area countries

1997   1998   1999   2000
                                        (estimate)

all the bonds are identical and that countries are jointly responsible for each other's debt. Indeed, the club's house rules (as per the Maastricht Treaty) explicitly state that no individual country will be 'bailed out' if it experiences difficulty in repaying its debt. Nevertheless, with all government debt in the same common currency of denomination, it gives rise to concerns that if one member ran into difficulties, any other debt in the same currency (i.e. the debt of the rest of the members) would look unattractive to the outside world.

Thus, a 60% debt ceiling is imposed – not only to prevent any single country from issuing excessive debt, but also to protect the club's good name as a whole.

The UK passes this test with ease. The recent budget surpluses have brought about a reduction in the stock of debt to little more than 40% of GDP, well below the 60% requirement. Again, not only does the UK pass the test by an ample margin, but it also compares well with the existing euro countries who, with an average stock of debt at 71% in 2000, actually exceeded the 60% limit. This may seem a rather odd situation and, strangely enough, it was the otherwise highly strict Maastricht Treaty which allowed it to happen. A caveat in the treaty permitted the admission of countries with debt levels above 60%, providing such levels were *"approaching 60% sufficiently quickly"*. Indeed, there is widespread

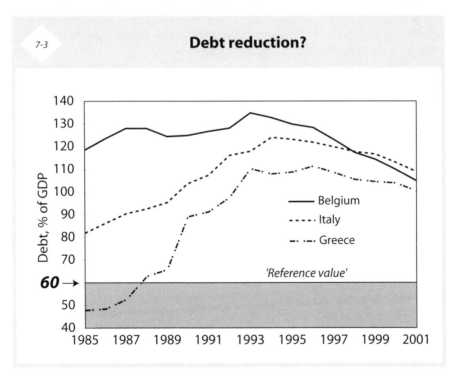

7-3

Debt reduction?

scepticism as to whether some of the countries admitted into the euro-area even met this loose caveat.

For example, between 1994 and 1997 (the year for which the requirement was assessed) Italy's debt stock had only fallen from 124% to 120% of GDP . Meanwhile, in Belgium, the pace of reduction was a shade faster but, even so, its debt stock in 1997 was still 123% of GDP. Furthermore, by 2001, these two countries will still have debt stocks in excess of 100% of GDP. More recently, Greece was judged to have passed the debt requirement, even though its stock of debt had also fallen very slowly and remained over 100% of GDP.

The UK's stock of debt has been consistently under 60% of GDP since 1985, so it has an established track record and, as long as the budget surpluses – or even small deficits – are recorded, the UK will more than meet this particular requirement for entry.

Inflation rate

Inflation is the subject of the third test. Any prospective member of the club must have an inflation rate that is low – and in line with existing euro-area countries This goes back to the 'one size fits all' regime mentioned earlier. Since the European Central Bank sets one interest rate for all the countries in the euro-area, and that rate is the principal weapon against inflation, the ECB needs to be quite sure that no country will enter with an inflation rate that is at odds with other countries in the euro-area. If, for example, the inflation rate in the euro-area was being maintained at its 2% target and a country with a 10% inflation rate joined, then it would practically impossible to set a rate that both protected growth for the existing member states and fought inflation in the newly-arrived country.

In the UK's case, a ceiling for the inflation rate is established with reference to the existing performance of euro-area countries. Specifically, the UK inflation rate must be no more than 1.5% higher than the average of the 'best three' euro-area countries. So, in October 2000, for example, the average inflation rate in the best three euro-area countries (Austria, France and Germany) was 2.2%. Adding 1.5% to that gives an inflation target of 3.7%. The UK inflation rate at the time was actually 0.9%, showing not only that the UK was well within target, but also that it had an inflation rate that was lower than any of the existing member countries. Furthermore, UK inflation has remained well within target throughout the last four years.

In Europe, there are two main measurements of inflation: The HICP, or 'Harmonized Index of Consumer Prices' and the more common RPI ('Retail Prices Index'). The HICP is the newer index and enables the

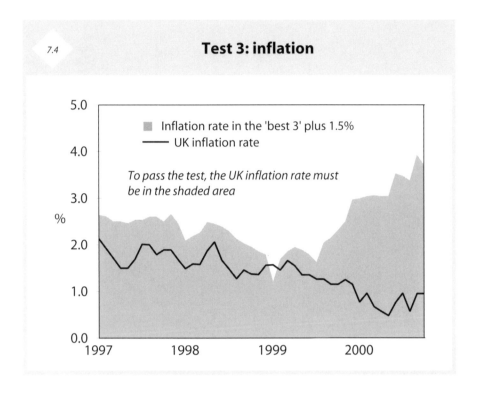

7.4

Test 3: inflation

- ▨ Inflation rate in the 'best 3' plus 1.5%
- — UK inflation rate

To pass the test, the UK inflation rate must be in the shaded area

inflation rate of all the EU countries to be calculated, as its name implies, in a harmonized way. Essentially, the principal differences between the two indices lies in the different treatment of housing costs and some other variations in coverage. Importantly, the indices employ different averaging methods for the price of individual goods which are included in the overall index, with the HICP using a geometric average and the RPI utilizing an arithmetic average. The interesting point here is that, using the newer (and perhaps more appropriate) HICP, the UK inflation rate is even lower than the figure revealed by the RPI index.

Once again, as with the previous three tests, the UK passes the inflation requirement by a comfortable margin and there is no reason to doubt that it will continue to do so in the coming years.

It should be noted here that, if the UK did join the euro-area, there would then be no national inflation target in the UK. Instead, this would be subsumed under the ECB's 2% inflation target for the entire euro-area.

Bond yield

The fourth test calls for any candidate country to demonstrate sufficiently low bond yields. The reason for this is that long-term bond yields are

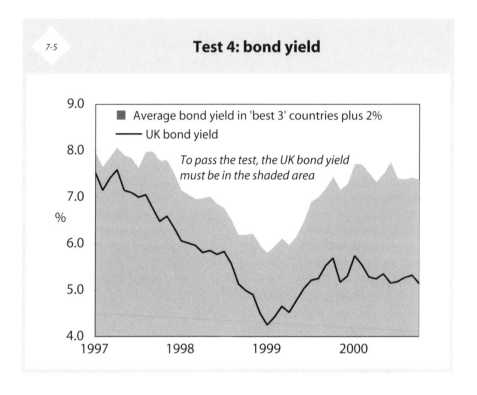

7-5

Test 4: bond yield

generally thought to be a good reflection of long-term inflation expectations. So, rather than judge a country's inflation performance solely on its latest data, as the inflation test does, the bond test indicates whether – in the view of the financial markets – the long-term outlook is really as rosy (or otherwise), as the current figures might suggest.

Just as the inflation test compares the UK to the three best inflation performances in the euro-area, so the test for bond yields compares the UK yield with the average bond yield in those same three countries. The target is that the UK's yield should not be more than 2% above that average.

For a recent example of the application of this test, let us look at the situation in October 2000. The average ten-year bond yield in Austria, France and Germany (the 'best three' inflation countries) was 5.4%, meaning that the UK bond yield needed to be less than 7.4%. In fact, the UK's yield was only 5.1% so, not only was it lower than the target, but it was also below the 'best three'. Indeed just as the yield target was comfortably met in October 2000, so it has been consistently throughout 2000 and, indeed over the course of the last four years.

With inflation expected to remain low in the UK, there is every reason for thinking this criterion will continue to be met in the coming years.

Exchange rate stability

We have seen that the first four Maastricht criteria outlined have all been comfortably met by the UK and the prognosis is that they will continue to be met quite easily over the next few years. However, the fifth, and last, criterion is another matter altogether.

As mentioned earlier, the criterion calls for the exchange rate of the applicant country to remain within the 'normal' fluctuation bands of the ERM for at least two years prior to entry – without major problems. Wim Duisenberg has clearly stated that there can be no exception to this rule for the UK.

The reason for this exchange rate requirement is simple. If a country were to join the euro, an unavoidable consequence would be the loss of exchange rate fluctuations against other euro-area countries – for ever. This is a major change. Indeed, as we emphasized in Chapter 1, it is the paramount effect of entry into European monetary union. Any prospective euro member country will clearly be better prepared for such a change if it has prior experience of smaller (or non-existent) exchange rate fluctuations against the euro-area.

7-6   The euro: a bigger deal for some than for others

Amongst the current twelve euro-area countries, six (Belgium, the Netherlands, Luxembourg, France, Austria and Germany – the 'core' bloc) had very limited exchange rate movements against each other for many years prior to the launch of the euro. It is principally due to these tight exchange rate linkages that their interest rates were also closely aligned and so, for these countries, moving to a single currency was arguably not such a big step. They had already become accustomed to exchange rate stability and shared broadly similar level of interest rates.

However, the other six countries in the euro-area – Italy, Spain, Portugal, Ireland, Finland and Greece – had experienced much greater historical exchange rate fluctuations *vis-à-vis* the core bloc. Furthermore, their currencies had tended to weaken against that bloc over time, reflecting the fact that, in general, they experienced higher levels of inflation. Looking at Figure 7-6, we can examine the average exchange rate change against the Deutschemark (taken as the benchmark currency) for the six-country core bloc, as well as the other (sometimes referred to as the 'peripheral') currencies. During the 1992/1993 and 1995 ERM crises, the exchange rates of these currencies weakened sharply against the core group. Naturally, as the countries joined the euro in 1999, the line becomes much flatter.

So how does the UK fit into this picture? Until the mid-1990s, sterling clearly had much in common with the group of weaker, peripheral currencies. Like Italy, Spain and Portugal, the UK also experienced severe problems emanating from the ERM crisis. However, more recently, sterling has strengthened against the euro-area currencies. Indeed, in late 2000, it was actually stronger against the Deutschemark than it had been in 1987. Sterling can no longer be classified as a weak, peripheral currency but, equally, it clearly does not deserve to be classified as a currency that can demonstrate a history of a stable exchange rate against the core European currencies.

Of course, exchange rate stability – as far as the Maastricht test is concerned – is based on exchange rate fluctuations *within* the Exchange Rate Mechanism. As an example, consider Italy's experience. In common with the UK, Italy left the Exchange Rate Mechanism (ERM) in September 1992 following a massive speculative attack against the currency. The intention was to rejoin the ERM 'soon', but this did not actually take place until November 1996. This meant that, by the time the euro was launched in January 1999, Italy had been in the ERM for the required time. However, there was a discrepancy, in that when the ECB and the European Commission published the *Convergence Reports* in March 1998 (which gave approval for the membership of Italy and others), Italy had actually only been back in the ERM for sixteen months.

It could be that this apparent discrepancy in Italy's admission may have set a precedent which, in turn, will benefit the UK. It is conceivable,

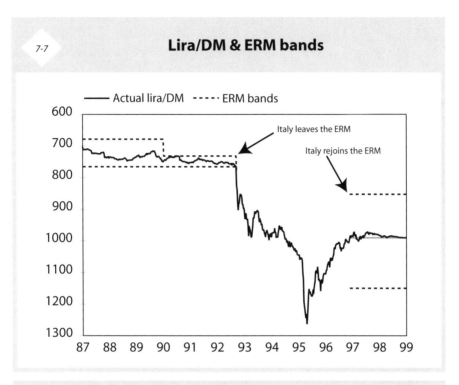

7-7

Lira/DM & ERM bands

—— Actual lira/DM   ----- ERM bands

Italy leaves the ERM

Italy rejoins the ERM

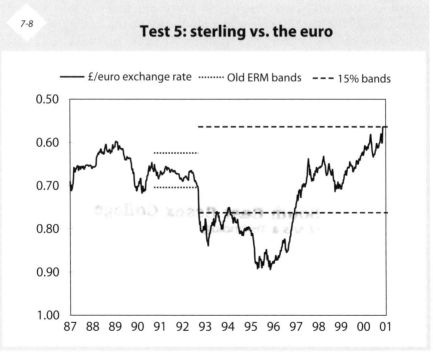

7-8

Test 5: sterling vs. the euro

—— £/euro exchange rate   ········ Old ERM bands   --- 15% bands

then, that Britain could spend less than two years in the ERM before it is approved for membership.

Furthermore, and despite Mr. Duisenberg's comments that no exceptions may be made for the UK, there have been suggestions that the ERM requirement should be scrapped altogether. One supporting argument is that, if sterling were to re-enter the ERM, it may swiftly become the target of the same speculative pressures that forced it out of the ERM in 1992. Indeed, this would indeed be the likely scenario if the foreign exchange markets reacted unfavourably to the prospect of the UK joining the euro-area.

It can also be argued that sterling's fluctuations in recent years have been no greater than those which would have been allowed in the ERM anyway. For example, if the 'old' ERM central rate had been maintained, and the fluctuation bands widened to +/-15% (as they were for most of the ERM currencies), sterling would have moved back within the bands in late 1996 and stayed within them ever since.

Conclusion

The UK easily meets four out of five of the Maastricht requirements for euro membership. Indeed, as far as these four requirements are concerned, the UK has a better performance than most of the current euro-area countries. Thus, if the UK wished to join the euro-area, it would be odd, to say the least, if any such application was blocked by a failure to meet the precise requirements of the fifth criterion – that of being an ERM member. In practice, it is likely that, if the UK did wish to join, some compromise on the ERM membership requirement would be sought, and possibly found.

8

What is the right exchange rate for joining the euro?

In the last chapter we noted that the fifth of the EU's tests for UK membership – the requirement that sterling should be in the Exchange Rate Mechanism for two years – was likely to be the most difficult for the UK to meet.

However, of even greater importance is the actual level of the exchange rate at which the UK might enter the euro. Since the launch of the euro in 1999, there have been repeated calls from UK industry that sterling is 'too strong' and that it is consequently difficult to operate competitively in the euro-area. There is no formal test of the exchange rate at which sterling should join the euro. Given that sterling's exchange rate against the euro (and, before that, against the Deutschemark and other European currencies) has been so volatile, it is difficult to identify a 'correct' exchange rate. However, since the entry rate would be irrevocable once the UK joined the euro, it is clearly of crucial importance.

Economists have the choice of three main methods to judge what is the 'right' exchange rate. Broadly – and this is actually quite unusual as economists are known for their inability to agree – they all suggest that an exchange rate of about 80 pence to one euro would be about right. That compares with an average exchange rate of 60 pence per euro during 2000. The implication is that sterling needs to fall in value by around a third.

'Right exchange rate' version 1: Big Mac Prices

The first measure is that which has been popularized by *The Economist* newspaper in recent years. It establishes the 'right' exchange rate by looking at the relative prices of McDonald's Big Mac™ hamburgers. This approach, which is based on what economists term the 'absolute' version of 'purchasing power parity' (PPP), states that a 'right' exchange rate between different countries should equalize prices in those countries. The theory works best if identical goods are chosen for comparison, hence the use of the Big Mac.

In its latest survey of Big Mac prices, *The Economist* found the average Big Mac price in the UK was £1.90, compared with an average price in the euro-area of €2.56. By applying a notional sterling/euro exchange rate of 74 pence to one euro (that is £1.90/€2.56) then the Big Mac would, on average, cost the same in the euro-area as in the UK.

However, there are complications. Chief among these is the fact that Big Mac prices vary within the euro-area: they are most expensive in France and cheapest in Spain. If the French Big Mac price is used as a basis in the calculation, the 'right' exchange rate would then become 67 pence to one euro; with the Spanish Big Mac price, the 'right' exchange rate would be 84 pence per euro.

8-1

1. The Big Mac method

Big Mac®

		Actual Big Mac price	Exchange rate: £1 to €1 that would equalize BigMac prices
	UK	£1.90	–
	France	€2.82	£0.67 to €1
	Germany	€2.55	£0.74 to €1
	Italy	€2.32	£0.82 to €1
	Spain	€2.25	£0.84 to €1
	Euro average	€2.56	£0.74 to €1

Source: 'The Economist, 25 April 2000
*'Big Mac' is a Registered Trademark of the McDonalds Corpoartion

---

One way of summarizing these differences in the euro-area is to say that, when using the *higher* French prices as a basis, sterling needs to be *stronger* in order for prices to be equalized and, conversely, when using the *lower* Spanish prices, sterling can be *weaker*.

Of course, using the price of a hamburger to set sterling's entry rate to the euro may be criticized as lacking financial sophistication! However, there are two other measures which are worthy of consideration: a measure of relative (rather than absolute) purchasing power parity; and a measure of sterling's 'equilibrium' exchange rate.

'Right exchange rate' version 2: Relative Purchasing Power Parity

The relative purchasing power parity view of exchange rates holds that *changes* in the exchange rate over time should reflect *changes* in relative prices. So, for example, if prices in the euro-area rise by 2.5% a year and prices in the UK rise by only 1.5% a year, sterling should appreciate against the euro by 1% per year. That exchange rate appreciation would then offset the higher prices in the euro-area, keeping relative prices the same.

The challenge in using this approach is to ensure that any changes in relative prices are assessed from a suitable 'starting point'. For example, in 1995, the exchange rate averaged 87 pence per euro while, in 1990, it averaged 68 pence per euro. Clearly any adjustment to these 'starting point' or 'base period' exchange rates to calculate relative price movements since then would result in different estimates of the 'right' exchange rate.

We can see, then, that the utmost care needs to be taken when selecting the appropriate base period. A reasonably sound case can be made for using early 1987. At that time, there was general agreement among the finance ministers from the seven leading industrial countries that most of the world's key exchange rates were fairly aligned with each other. The earlier overvaluation of the dollar had been corrected while, in Europe, a realignment of the Exchange Rate Mechanism in February 1987 had also restored exchange rates among the member countries to those which fairly represented absolute purchasing power parity (that is, they were in line with the 'right' exchange rates on the basis of version one, above).

Figure 8-2 shows the trend in the euro-sterling exchange rate since 1987 which would reflect the relative movement in prices. (A range of different prices measures are utilized – consumer prices, export prices, producer prices and relative wage costs. Note that the euro exchange rate is based on the Deutschemark prior to 1999, while prices are based on the Deutschemark prior to 1999 and the euro thereafter.) The overall trend is for sterling to depreciate – that is, for one euro to buy more pounds sterling – and this reflects the relatively higher UK inflation rate experienced in the past. As UK inflation declined in the mid-1990s the downward trend slowed. More recently, the PPP exchange rate has been

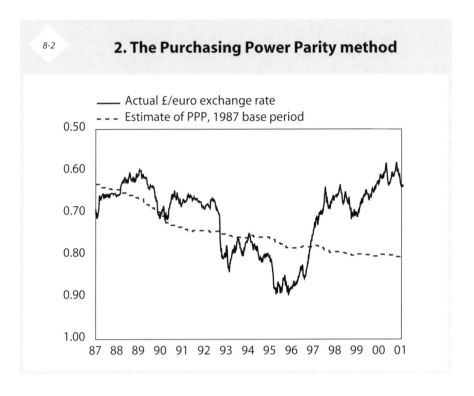

8-2

2. The Purchasing Power Parity method

——— Actual £/euro exchange rate
- - - Estimate of PPP, 1987 base period

reasonably stable, reflecting the fact that there is little difference between UK and euro-area inflation.

The relationship between sterling's actual exchange rate and the PPP trend is actually very useful in interpreting sterling's movements since the late 1980s. In particular:

- Nigel Lawson's policy of capping sterling, from March 1987 to March 1988, at DM3.000/£ (equivalent to 65 pence per euro in the chart) can be seen as an attempt to keep sterling too weak (its PPP rate at the time was over DM3.000 to £1).

- When sterling joined the ERM in October 1990, it was at an overvalued exchange rate. The central rate in the ERM was DM2.95/£, equivalent to 66 pence per euro, whereas the PPP exchange rate was DM2.67/£, equivalent to 73 pence per euro).

- Sterling remained overvalued throughout its two-year period in the ERM, which ended in September 1992. This goes some way to explain the depth of the UK recession at that time.

- When sterling was forced out of the ERM in 1992, its exchange rate initially fell to around its PPP level, but then declined to a low-point, in late 1995, of 90 pence per euro, at which time sterling was significantly undervalued.

- At less than 60 pence per euro in late 2000, sterling was overvalued against the euro by as much as 25%.

Right exchange rate version 3: Fundamental Equilibrium Exchange Rate (FEER)

A third method, the 'Fundamental Equilibrium Exchange Rate' (FEER), takes several other factors into account in determining the 'right' exchange rate. The aim is to identify the exchange rate that will bring both internal and external balance to an economy. Internal balance means that the economy is operating at around its full capacity: in particular, it is normally taken to mean that the unemployment rate is close to its 'natural' level, although identifying such a level proves to be rather difficult in practice. External balance means that if a country is running a current account deficit, for example, then this is equally balanced by a long-term capital inflow (for example, from inward investment direct

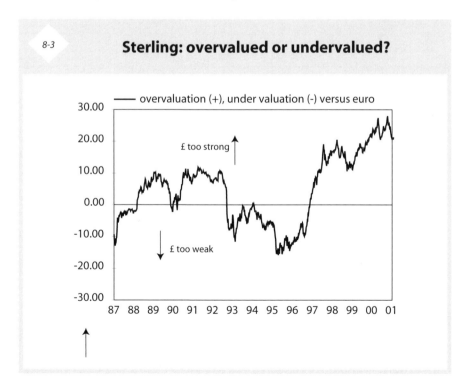

8-3

Sterling: overvalued or undervalued?

investment, such as happens when a Japanese car firm builds a manufacturing plant in the UK).

Estimates of such FEERs rely on sophisticated modelling of the economy. With different models producing varying results, and diverse assumptions as to what constitutes internal and external balance, it is clear that different FEER estimates can result. Nevertheless, a recent comprehensive study, which was conducted by the founders of the FEER concept (the Institute for International Economics in Washington DC), estimated the 'right' euro-sterling rate to be around 85 pence per euro.

8-4	The three 'right' rates
Method:	**'Right' exchange rate:**
1: Big Mac	
France	67p to €1
Germany	74p to €1
Italy	82p to €1
Spain	84p to €1
Average of four countries	74p to €1
2: Relative PPP	80p to €1
3: Equilibrium Exchange rate	85p to €1
Average of all three methods	80p to €1

Summary of results on the 'right' exchange rate

Clearly, the three measures examined in this chapter result in a range of estimates for the 'right' exchange sterling-euro rate. However, they each share something in common and that is they all judge sterling, in early 2001, to be significantly overvalued against the euro. An exchange rate of about 80 pence to one euro would seem to be 'about right'.

This conclusion is supported by a range of anecdotal evidence from both exporters and importers in the UK, as well as British holidaymakers

8-5	A 'wrong' exchange rate: the consequences

Overvalued	Undervalued
· **Harder** conditions **for UK exporters:** if £ prices unchanged, euro prices rise *or* profit margins on exports suffer	· **Easier** conditions **for UK exporters:** if £ prices unchanged, euro prices fall *or* profit margins on exports improve
· **Imports** from euro area **cheaper**	· **Imports** from euro area **more expensive**
· **Holidays** in euro area **cheaper**	· **Holidays** in euro area **more expensive**

in the euro-area. In short, sterling needs to fall in value substantially if the UK is not to join the euro at a disadvantageous exchange rate.

9

Are two tests enough?

Gordon Brown's tests and the EU's tests, between them, cover a large number of aspects of the relative performance of the UK and euro-area economies. However, there are still potential pitfalls. For example, it may be that the UK could technically pass the tests, but would still be unsuitable for joining the euro. Alternatively, it could fail the tests and be prevented from joining when, in reality, it would be an entirely suitable candidate. In this chapter, we look at other a range of issues which, if taken into account, would considerably enhance the testing procedure.

The IoD's tests

The UK IoD (Institute of Directors) has proposed its own version of the government's five tests. These appear both to add precision to Gordon Brown's criteria and introduce new yardsticks.

Convergence with the eurozone, not the US

The first IoD test specifies more precisely what should be understood by Gordon Brown's first test of 'sustainable convergence'. The IoD suggests that the correlation between UK and eurozone economic growth should be higher than that between UK and US GDP growth for a period of ten years. This would provide reassurance that the UK was more closely linked to the eurozone than the US, which is not the case at present indeed has not been so for the last decade. In fact, it could be argued that the IoD's test is insufficiently tight. For example, the UK economy had a higher correlation with the eurozone than with the US in the 1980s, but this situation was reversed in the 1990s. So, even a ten-year long correlation may not be long enough to judge whether the UK and eurozone economies have sufficiently converged with each other.

9-1

The IoD's five tests

**The UK Institute of Directors' tests of whether it would
be suitable for the UK to join the euro are:**

1   GDP correlation coefficient with eurozone should be higher than with the US for a decade.

2   Eurozone should account for more than 50% of current account earnings for a sustained period.

3   Proportion of UK fixed rate mortgages (currently 25%) should converge with France and Germany (about 95%).

4   Eurozone unemployment should fall to UK levels and the eurozone proportion of the population employed should rise to UK levels.

5   The gap between eurozone and UK tax revenues as a proportion of GDP should fall from 6% to 3%.

Foreign earnings

The second IoD test calls for most of the UK's current account earnings to come from the euro-area. At present, it is not quite met (the proportion was 48.6% in 1999), but there is an upward trend in the share. This test should be seen as providing extra reassurance with regard to the closeness of the link between the UK and the eurozone.

Mortgage market

The third IoD requirement is that the importance of fixed rate mortgages in the UK should be similar to that in France and Germany. Currently, this test is nowhere near being met as 25% of UK mortgages are at fixed rates compared with 95% in both France and Germany. However, the growing proportion of *new* mortgages at fixed rates in the UK means that the share of the outstanding stock will rise over time. Clearly, this will only happen quite slowly and thus it seems highly unlikely that the required proportion will be met for a very long time.

The importance of this requirement is that, if the UK has a larger proportion of mortgages at variable rates of interest, UK households are more susceptible to short-term interest rates changes. Changes in short-term interests rates by the ECB would, if the UK joined the euro, have an effect on UK variable rate mortgages, just as they are affected now by a change in the Bank of England's interest rate. Fixed rate mortgage payments would not, of course, change as a result. In a nutshell, UK households would suffer more if the ECB pushed up short-term interest rates (and benefit more if it reduced interest rates) then would households in the rest of the eurozone.

Labour market

The IoD also wishes to see the unemployment rate in the eurozone coming closer to the UK level, with the proportion of people employed rising to the UK level. The differences between the UK and eurozone rates are currently about 4% and 15%, respectively.

Tax shares

Finally, the IoD wishes to see the gap between tax revenues narrower than at present. Overall tax revenues as a share of the economy are currently 6% higher in the UK than the eurozone. The IoD wants to see this difference cut to no more than 3%.

Overall assessment

There is no doubt that it would be desirable for the IoD's requirements to be met. However, in reality, it is somewhat unlikely that they could be met in anything but the very long term. Paradoxically, it may be very hard to meet some of them unless the UK first joins the euro! For example, becoming a part of the eurozone would probably act as a catalyst for change in the mortgage market, helping the proportion of fixed rate mortgages rise. It may also help in the process of economic convergence.

The general flexibility and competitiveness of the UK and eurozone economies

The IoD's tests relate primarily to a comparison of economic conditions in the UK and the eurozone. However, it is arguably of even more importance that the overall structure, flexibility and competitiveness of the UK and the eurozone should be similar.

9-2	**Overall competitiveness rankings**	
Ranking	Overall rating	Country
1	100.0	USA
2	75.2	Singapore
3	68.5	Switzerland
4	63.9	Sweden
5	63.5	Iceland
6	63.4	Canada
7	63.4	Denmark
8	63.1	Australia
9	60.5	Hong Kong
10	59.4	UK
11	57.8	Norway
12	57.4	Japan
13	**57.1**	**Eurozone**

Source: based on IMD data but aggregating Eurozone countries

One attempt to measure these factors is made each year in the World Competitiveness Scoreboard (see Figure 9-2), which is produced by the International Institute for Management Development (IMD) in Lausanne, Switzerland. A country's level of competitiveness is assessed on the basis of economic and statistical data, as well as survey data. The survey data relate to responses to questions such as:

- whether bureaucracy hinders business development;
- the ease of new business creation;
- the availability and competence of senior management;
- the creation of shareholder value by companies;
- working days lost through industrial disputes;
- whether firms are customer orientated;
- whether there s a general entrepreneurial environment;
- whether ethical practices are implemented in companies.

Scores range from 100 (the most competitive) to 0 (least competitive). In the year 2000, the US (which sets the benchmark for all countries) scored 100 while Russia, the lowest ranked, scored 5.

In aggregate, the eurozone economies rank below the UK. Moreover, the other two countries that have decided not to join the euro-area (Sweden and Denmark) rank relatively highly, as do three European countries that are not members of the EU (Switzerland, Norway and Iceland).

Within the eurozone there are substantial differences in competitiveness. Finland, the Netherlands and Ireland rank the highest, with Spain, Portugal and Greece coming bottom.

The UK also ranks better than Germany and France in terms of the number of people involved in new business start-ups, another indication of the overall flexibility of the economy.

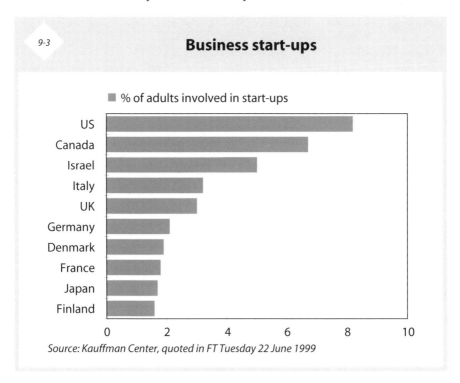

9-3

Business start-ups

Source: Kauffman Center, quoted in FT Tuesday 22 June 1999

Regional differences

The north-south divide in the UK receives regular media attention. It is represented in a number of different ways – variations in house prices, unemployment rates, and so on – but perhaps the best overall measure is

9-4

Regional differences in the UK

■ GDP per head in UK regions

Northern Ireland
North East
Wales
Yorkshire & the Humber
North West
West Midlands
South West
East Midlands
Scotland
UK average
East
South East
Greater London

40   60   80   100   120   140   160   180

1998, index, UK average = 100

Source: Regional Trends, No 35, The Stationery Office

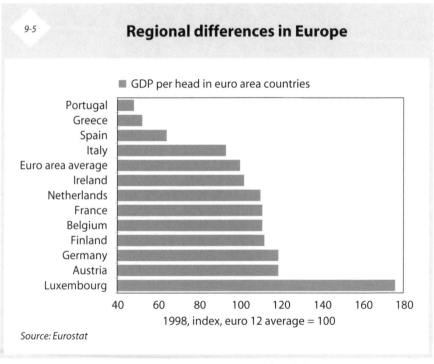

9-5

Regional differences in Europe

■ GDP per head in euro area countries

Portugal
Greece
Spain
Italy
Euro area average
Ireland
Netherlands
France
Belgium
Finland
Germany
Austria
Luxembourg

40   60   80   100   120   140   160   180

1998, index, euro 12 average = 100

Source: Eurostat

overall economic output, or gross domestic product (GDP) per head. Figure 9-4 shows that Greater London is the most prosperous region, with income per head 30% higher than the UK average; North East England and Wales are 21%, and Northern Ireland 24%, below average.

These differences between regions in the UK are much *smaller* than the differences between different countries in the eurozone (see Figure 9-5). Luxembourg is the most prosperous eurozone country with GDP per head 76% above average, followed by Austria and Germany at 19% above average. Greece and Portugal are the least well-off, at around one half the average.

In the UK, regional differences have tended to widen over time, becoming more marked over the last twenty-five years. There is a concern that the eurozone differences may similarly widen over time. One reason for expecting this is that the combination of the EU single market and the use of a single currency will allow companies to operate more effectively on a pan-European basis. This will aid distribution and mean that production can be more easily centralized, with associated economies of scale. As an example, in the USA, car production is highly centralized in the MidWest (see Figure 9-6). If this example were followed in the eurozone, car production may be centralized in, say, Germany (see Figure 9-7). Extending the argument further, each country

9-6

US car production

% in each region, 1995

MidWest	68
South	23
North East	6
West	4

Source: Oxford Economic Forecasting

9-7

European car production

% in each region, 1996-7

Germany	38
France	27
Italy	12
Spain	16

Source: Oxford Economic Forecasting

would specialize in what it does best: Finland would produce mobile phones, Ireland would turn out computer software, and Spain and Portugal could become golf courses!

Conclusions

The IoD's tests are useful in that they help to refine – and make more objective – Gordon Brown's tests. But they may be so hard to satisfy that the UK would never fulfil the requirements for joining!

Other tests indicate that the UK has a more flexible economy than the eurozone. In this sense, it may be more appropriate to think of the UK joining when the *eurozone's* flexibility has increased.

Finally, there is a concern that the regional differences in the eurozone may cause problems in the future. Currently, the gap between the prosperity levels of different countries in the eurozone is wider than the north-south divide in the UK. If the single currency encourages industries to become more concentrated in certain regions, such gaps could widen still further.

10

The Bank of England and the ECB

We have already noted that, if the UK joins the euro, then interest rates in the UK will be set by the European Central Bank (ECB) and the UK's official interest rates will be the same as those in all other euro-area countries. This chapter explores the changes that would be involved in moving to such a system. We start by looking at the present structures and operating techniques of both central banks.

How the Bank of England sets UK interest rates

The Bank of England's Monetary Policy Committee (MPC), which comprises nine members (see Figure 10-1), is the body responsible for deciding the level of UK interest rates.

The MPC meets on the Wednesday and Thursday following the first Monday of each month. Discussions on the current level of interest rates take place at the meeting and, if any changes are made, they are normally announced at midday on the second day of the meeting (i.e. noon on Thursday). Decisions to alter interest rates are taken on the basis of one man one vote, with the governor having the casting vote.

The main factor taken into account in deciding the level of UK interest rates is the MPC's forecast of inflation. The target inflation rate is set by the Treasury and the Bank of England then endeavours to meet the target by taking appropriate action. Currently, the Treasury's target is 2.5% for *underlying* RPI inflation, commonly referred to as 'RPIX' ('underlying' means that the effect of mortgage interest payments is excluded). It is not surprising, therefore, that the MPC's forecast of inflation is regarded as the single most significant indicator of all among those which are considered when setting the level of UK interest rates.

10-1   **The Bank of England's MPC...**

THREADNEEDLE STREET, LONDON

307th year!

The

Bank of England

STARRING

SIR EDWARD
GEORGE   *Governor of the Bank of England*

Term of office: Five years, expiring on 30 June 2003
Career: "Eddie" George joined the Bank of England in 1962 after graduating from
               Cambridge University in Economics. He has been seconded from the Bank of
               England to Moscow State University to study Russian, to work as an economist in
               the Bank for International Settlements, Basle and to the IMF. He was appointed
               deputy governor in 1990 and has been governor since 1993.

SUPPORTED BY

MERVYN
KING   *Deputy Governor, responsible for monetary policy*

Term of office: Five years, expiring on 31 May 2003
Career: Before becoming deputy governor he was the Bank of England's chief
               economist, from March 1991. Prior to that he was professor of economics at the
               London School of Economics.

DAVID
CLEMENTI   *Deputy Governor, responsible for financial stability*

Term of office: Five years, expiring on 31 August 2002
Career: Before joining the Bank, he worked at Kleinwort Benson for 22 years, playing a
               leading role in the UK privatisation programme. At the Bank he has been heavily
               involved in helping the City prepare for the single currency

IAN
PLENDERLEITH   *Executive Director, responsible for financial market operations*

Term of office: Three years, expiring on 31 May 2002
Career: He joined the Bank of England in 1965. He has been seconded to the
               International Monetary Fund; has been an alternate director of the European
               Investment Bank, Luxembourg, and is currently an alternate director of the Bank
               for International Settlements, Basle.

...rave reviews so far!

CHARLES
BEAN *Executive Director and Chief Economist*

Term of office: From 1 October 2000 to 31 May 2001
Career: After a spell in the UK Treasury, he joined the London School of Economics as a
           lecturer in 1982, rising to professor in 1990 and head of department in 1999. He
           has published widely in academic journals, particularly on monetary policy,
           European Monetary Union and European unemployment and economic growth.

CHRISTOPER
ALLSOPP *Monetary Policy Committee Member*

Term of office: Three years, expiring on 31 May 2003
Career: He was an Oxford University economist before joining the MPC. He had
           previously worked as an economist at the OECD and in the Bank of England.

STEPHEN
NICKELL *Monetary Policy Committee Member*

Term of office: Three years, expiring on 31 May 2003
Career: He is a part-time member of the MPC and also part-time professor of economics
           at the London School of Economics. His academic career has included being
           professor of economics and the director of the Institute of Economics and
           Statistics, University of Oxford, and a professorial fellow of Nuffield College,
           Oxford.

DR. SUSHIL
WADHWANI *Monetary Policy Committee Member*

Term of office: Three years, expiring on 31 May 2002
Career: He is a full-time member of the MPC. He had previously held a number of City
           positions, at a hedge fund and at Goldman Sachs. Before that he was a lecturer in
           economics at the London School of Economics.

DR. DEANNE
JULIUS *Executive Director and Chief Economist*

Term of office: Three years, expiring on 31 May 2001
Career: She is a full-time member of the MPC. Before that she held a number of positions
           in the private sector, including chief economist of British Airways and chief
           economist of the Royal Dutch Shell Group.

The factors taken into account in the MPC inflation forecast are set out in the Bank of England's quarterly *Inflation Report*, and include:

- growth of money supply and credit
- house prices
- equity prices
- wage developments
- productivity trends
- oil prices
- commodity prices
- the sterling exchange rate

Clearly, the nine MPC members often have divergent views on the likely course of inflation. This reflects their different opinions on: how the economy works, the expected movements in sterling's exchange rate, trends in wages, productivity, oil prices, and so on. In recent years, for example, there has been an ongoing debate about the influence of technological change on the economy. Some have argued that this allows faster economic growth and lower inflation than was possible in the past — thus making a case for keeping interest rates lower than would otherwise be the case.

As there is no one single view about the likely trend in inflation, the MPC publishes a 'fan chart' which shows a range of forecasts for the future inflation rate, with various probabilities. Because changes in interest rates made by the MPC can take a year or two to impact on inflation, attention is normally focused on the MPC's forecast for two years ahead.

It is a matter of public record (see below) that the MPC's monthly meetings entail considerable detailed discussion on the various economic data which are presented, before any proposal is formulated and put to the vote.

How open and transparent is the Bank of England?

The Bank of England ranks highly in terms of its openness and transparency. In particular:

- its forecasts for inflation are published on a quarterly basis and normally receive a good deal of attention in the financial press and media;

- the minutes of the MPC meetings are also published, two weeks after each meeting;
- the way in which the MPC committee members vote on interest rates is disclosed in the minutes;
- MPC members frequently give speeches on monetary policy and economic issues;
- MPC members regularly provide evidence to Parliamentary Select Committees;
- MPC members' credentials are examined before a Parliamentary Committee before they are appointed.
- The governor of the Bank of England must explain, in a letter to the chancellor of the exchequer, any deviation of more than 1% either side of the inflation target. Since this procedure started in 1997, inflation has remained very close to its 2.5% target. No letters have been written!

How successful has the Bank of England been?

In 1997, the Bank was given independence to set interest rates and, since then, it has been remarkably successful in keeping inflation under control – indeed, the level has hardly strayed from its 2.5% target. This is particularly remarkable given that the UK's history reveals a rather dismal track record when it comes to keeping inflation in check. Of course, the Bank of England could claim, with some justification, that this poor record reflects the fact that, prior to its independence in 1997, the process of setting interest rates was subject to heavy political influence. Now, the rates which are set are solely based on economic indicators. Critics claim, however, that the Bank of England has merely been lucky as, in recent years, there has been low inflation throughout much of the industrialized world.

The Bank has also faced criticism over its policy of maintaining relatively high interest rates. Although inflation has stayed low, the knock-on effect of high interest rates has been a relatively strong value of sterling, particularly against the euro. This, in turn, has been detrimental to UK exporters in Europe.

On balance, however, there seems little doubt that, since gaining its independence, the Bank of England has been remarkably successful in pursuing its main objective of low and stable inflation.

The ECB (European Central Bank)

The ECB was established on 1 June 1998 and, on 1 January 1999, it became responsible for setting interest rates for the 11 countries of the euro-area.

The structure of the ECB

The main decision-making body of the ECB is the Governing Council. It consists of the six members of the Executive Board and the 12 governors of the national central banks of the euro-area (see Figure 10-2).

Formally, all the members of the Executive Board were appointed by 'common accord of the Heads of State or Government' of the eleven founder countries of the euro-area. Rather less formally, there was disagreement about who should be the first president of the ECB. In particular, the French wanted the president to be French and duly nominated Jean-Claude Trichet, governor of the Banque de France. In the end, a compromise was hammered out at the Brussels summit of 1-4 May 1998, whereby Wim Duisenberg (a Dutchman) was appointed for a non-renewable eight-year term (although it was announced that he had made a 'voluntary' declaration that he would step down after four years). The Brussels summit also agreed that Mr Duisenberg's successor would be a Frenchman and 'noted' that President Chirac had formally proposed Mr Trichet for this post. Interestingly, in a number of newspaper interviews on 31 December 1998 (the eve of the launch of the euro), Mr Duisenberg denied the existence of any agreement that he would step down halfway through his tenure.

How the ECB sets euro-area interest rates

Like the Bank of England's Monetary Policy Committee, the ECB's Governing Council also sets interest rates on the basis of 'one man, one vote', with the president having the casting vote. These votes are taken at meetings which are normally held every two weeks at the ECB's head office in Frankfurt (although they can also be held be teleconference). Typically, twice a year, the meetings take place in one of the euro-area member countries (for example, in 2000, meetings were hosted by the Bank of Spain in Madrid and by the Bank of France in Paris). Two main factors are taken into account in deciding on the level of interest rates. First, the growth of the money supply plays a prominent role. A 'reference value' for the growth of M3 (a broad measure of the money supply which includes cash in circulation, most bank deposits with a maturity of less than two years and also other money market instruments) is set. Since the ECB was established in 1999, this reference value has been set at 4.5 %, although M3 growth has consistently exceeded this level. The rationale for setting a monetary target is that faster monetary growth can be expected to lead to higher inflation in the future and it is likely that this above-target growth of M3 has been a factor in prompting the ECB to raise interest rates.

Secondly, the ECB takes into account a broad range of other factors that are likely to affect the outlook for inflation in the euro-area. These indicators include wages, the exchange rate, long-term interest rates, various measures of economic activity, fiscal policy indicators, price and cost indices, and business and consumer surveys.

Like the Bank of England, the ECB has a target for inflation – currently 2% – for the euro-area as a whole. In the first year of the ECB's existence, this target was easily met, but the combination of rising oil prices and a weakening of the value of the euro resulted in the target being exceeded from mid-2000 onwards. Most economists believe that the factors behind the increase are largely temporary in nature and that inflation will therefore start to fall back in line again. Nevertheless, the way that the ECB tackles this target overshoot will be an important test of the Bank's credibility in conducting monetary policy for the euro-area.

How open and transparent is the ECB?

The ECB has faced a good deal of criticism regarding the transparency of its operations. In particular, the minutes of its Governing Council meetings are not published. Mr Duisenberg famously commented that these might be published "after seventeen years" – perhaps because this would be after the terms of office of two consecutive ECB presidents. When criticized for this non-publication, the ECB usually puts forward the same argument, the gist of which being that if the minutes were made public then there would be undue pressure placed on national central bank governors to vote in a particular way.

How successful has the ECB been?

Given that the ECB has only been existence for just over two years, it is arguably too early to pass judgement on its performance. However, in the financial markets, there have been real doubts about the Bank's credibility thus far. The main concerns seem to centre on the value of the euro. Almost from birth, the currency showed consistent weakness against the US dollar, and yet little ECB activity was seen.

As we noted earlier, there has also been concern that inflation in 2000 exceeded the 2% target level, although this overshoot is partially

The ECB on show in Frankfurt...

KAISERSTRASSE, FRANKFURT

3rd year!

The

European Central Bank

STARRING

WILLEM F.
DUISENBERG   *President of the ECB*

Term of office: Eight years, expiring on 31 May 2006
Career: From 1997 he was president of the European Monetary Institute, the forerunner of the ECB. Before that he had been president of the Dutch central bank for fifteen years.

SUPPORTED BY

CHRISTIAN
NOYER   *Vice-president of the ECB*

Term of office: Four years, expiring on 31 May 2002
Career: Mainly in the French Treasury and the French Ministry for Economic Affairs, Finance and Industry.

SIRKKA
HÄMÄLÄINEN   *Executive Board member of the ECB*

Term of office: Five years, expiring on 31 May 2003
Career: Almost entirely in the Bank of Finland, of which she was governor from 1992-1998.

TOMMASO
PADOA-SCHIOPPA   *Executive Board member of the ECB*

Term of office: Seven years, expiring on 31 May 2005
Career: Mainly in the Bank of Italy, where he was deputy director general from 1984 to 1997. Most of his career at the Bank of Italy has been in the research department. He spent four years in Brussels (1979-1983) as director-general for Economic and Financial Affairs at the European Commission.

..and on tour twice a year

EUGENIO
DOMINGO SOLANS   *Executive Board member of the ECB*

Term of office: Six years, expiring on 31 May 2004.
Career: Mainly as an economist and board member of several Spanish private sector
               banks. He was a member of the Governing Council of the Bank of Spain for four
               years from 1994-1998.

OTMAR
ISSING   *Executive Board member of the ECB*

Term of office: Three years, expiring on 31 May 2003
Career: As an academic economist as well as in the German Economics Ministry. At the
               Bundesbank, he was a board member from 1990 to 1998. He is generally
               regarded as the ECB's chief economist.

ALSO APPEARING ON THE GOVERNING COUNCIL

Guy
QUADEN
Governor, National Bank of Belgium

Ernst
WELTEKE
President, Deutsche Bundesbank

Lucas D.
PAPADEMOS
Governor, Bank of Greece

Jaime
CARUANA
Governor, Bank of Spain

Jean-Claude
TRICHET
Governor, Bank of France

Maurice
O'CONNELL
Governor, Central Bank of Ireland

Antonio
FAZIO
Governor, Bank of Italy

Yves
MERSCH
Governor, Central Bank of Luxembourg

Nout
WELLINK
President, Dutch Central Bank

Klaus
LIEBSCHER
Governor, Central Bank of Austria

Vítor Manuel Ribeiro
CONSTÂNCIO
Governor, Bank of Portugal

Matti
VANHALA
Governor, Central Bank of Finland

attributable to the rise in oil prices. However, the ECB's response to the inflationary pressure was to hike interest rates – a move which was criticized by many as it threatened to put a brake on the resurgence in European economic growth (which was languishing far behind that of the US).

There is ongoing concern about the wisdom of a 'one-size-fits-all' approach to interest rates (i.e. there is one level of interest rates for all eleven of the euro-area countries). Critics claim that, inevitably, this is leading to interest rates being set too high for those countries with slower growth and little evidence of inflation; and too low for the smaller European economies (such as Ireland) which have exhibited very strong growth and inflationary pressures.

What would be the main changes if the ECB set interest rates for the UK economy?

In many senses, the Bank of England and the ECB are similar. Both are quite independent of government and both have a clear mandate to keep inflation low. However, some significant changes would result if the UK joined the euro-area:

- The MPC would no longer have the power to set UK interest rates. Interest rates for the UK and all the other economies in the euro-area would be set by the ECB.

- The MPC may well be disbanded, although it could remain as an advisory body to the Bank of England.

- The UK Treasury would no longer set a UK inflation target. This would be prohibited under ECB requirements for all euro-area central banks to be free of such influence from national governments. The only relevant inflation target would be that for the entire euro-area.

- A forecast of UK inflation would almost certainly still be produced but, if UK inflation threatened to move higher, it could only be offset by a rise in ECB interest rates.

- On the ECB Governing Council, the Bank of England would have one seat and thus a single vote. There would be twelve other central bank governors and six Executive Board members also voting on interest rates.

- Minutes of meetings of the Governing Council would not be published (unlike the minutes of MPC meetings which are freely available).

Mr Duisenberg currently gives evidence on ECB policy only before the European Parliament, not national parliaments. He has refused, for example, to give evidence before the French National Assembly.

The governor of the Bank of England would, of course, still give evidence on ECB actions to the UK Parliament.

Conclusions

Handing over responsibility for setting UK interest rates to the ECB is a move that no UK government could ever take lightly. The Bank of England has enjoyed great success in recent years in keeping inflation low and stable. Furthermore, the openness of its decision-making and the transparency of its operations compare favourably with the ECB.

11

The road ahead

If the UK is to join the euro, three distinct timetables govern when such an event could take place. These relate to:

- the sequence of decisions that have to be made in the UK;
- the sequence of decisions that have to be made by various European Union bodies;
- the time needed to prepare for, and then implement, the changeover from sterling to the euro.

Each of the three timetables, which are illustrated in Figure 11-1, has three distinct stages and these are discussed below. However, the clock will not start ticking on any of the three timetables shown unless the present Labour administration is returned to power at the forthcoming general election. Should the Conservative Party form the next government, they have made it plain that they will 'keep the pound', at least for the next parliamentary term.

The sequence of decisions in the UK

Tony Blair, the prime minister, has pledged that, if Labour wins the next election, an assessment of Gordon Brown's five tests for joining the euro will be made within the first two years in office. It is widely regarded that the political decision to join has already been taken, as long as Mr Brown's economic tests are met. The assessment of whether or not the tests are indeed met, will be made by the UK Treasury.

If it turns out that the UK fails to meet any of these tests, a re-examination could take place at a later date. However, as most of the evidence used to apply the tests changes only gradually over time, the reassessment could not reasonably take place for several years.

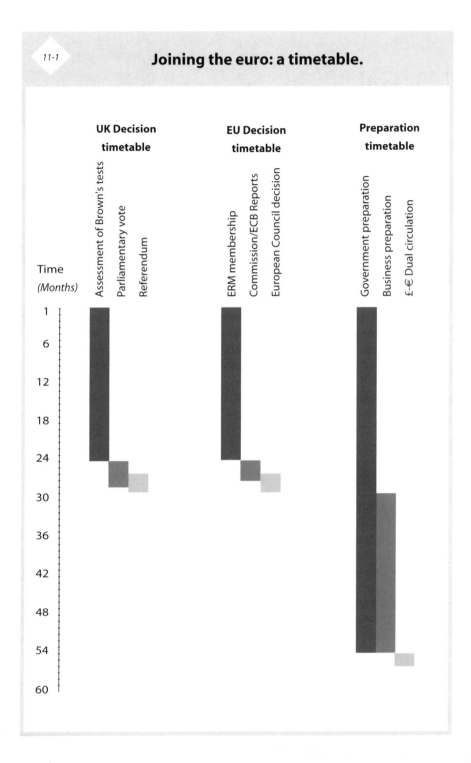

11-1

Joining the euro: a timetable.

UK Decision timetable

Assessment of Brown's tests

Parliamentary vote

Referendum

EU Decision timetable

ERM membership

Commission/ECB Reports

European Council decision

Preparation timetable

Government preparation

Business preparation

£–€ Dual circulation

Time
(Months)

1
6
12
18
24
30
36
42
48
54
60

11-2   **Danish referendum: main arguments**

YES supporters   **NO** supporters

- It would remove currency swings
- It would boost Denmark's influence in the EU
- Euro would help the economy

- Erosion of sovereignty
- Increase in European bureaucracy
- Welfare cutbacks

Assuming, however, that the tests were passed, then the government would formally recommend joining the euro. This would be followed by a vote in Parliament and a referendum. These three stages are sometimes dubbed collectively as the 'triple lock' on the UK joining the euro.

The government has indicated that there would be a gap of about four months between an entry recommendation and the of the subsequent referendum. This is significant because, while opinion polls have consistently showed that a strong majority would vote against joining in a referendum held now, optimistic 'europhiles' point to the fact that in the referendum on UK membership of the European Community in 1972 there was a substantial 'No' to 'Yes' swing in the run-up to voting day. However, the experience of the Danish referendum in September 2000 – the outcome of which was a rejection of euro membership – provides a very contrasting example. Indeed, three aspects of the Danish referendum are noteworthy.

- First, although it was a referendum on euro area membership, many voters seemed to vote on the basis of a wider set of factors relating to the role of the EU. Clearly, such a risk exists in the UK.

- Second, the pro-joining lobby received widespread support from the business community and the media. Opinion in the UK is undoubtedly more diverse.

- Third, Denmark has much closer linkages to the euro area than the UK.

Given these considerations, it is fair to say that a referendum would likely be the greatest obstacle to UK membership of the eurozone.

Again, assuming a return of the Labour government, it should be noted that Mr Brown's tests will be assessed *within* two years, and thus the overall length of this decision-making timetable (as far as the UK itself is concerned) would probably not exceed two years in total.

The EU's decision timetable

The European Commission and the European Central Bank will both produce reports on whether the UK satisfies the requirements for joining the euro. The ECB, in particular, has emphasized that the UK needs to be a member of the Exchange Rate Mechanism for two years before it will be allowed to join the euro. This may mean that the reports would not be written until the last few months of such a two-year period – and, conceivably, later still. An exception was made for Italy, which was approved for membership in March 1998, even though it had re-entered the ERM only sixteen months earlier. It is neither certain that such a lenient approach would be used for the UK, nor whether it would be in the UK's interests.

Assuming that the ECB and European Commission Convergence Reports on the UK are favourable, formal approval of the UK's membership would then be needed at a European Council meeting (that is, a meeting of the EU countries' heads of government). A special European Council meeting took place in Brussels in May 1998 to approve the original eurozone members. It would be possible, although unlikely, for such a special Council meeting to be convened to approve UK entry to the euro area. More likely, approval would take place at one of the regularly scheduled meetings. These take place towards the end of a country's six-month presidential term. For example, Greece's euro-area membership was approved in June 2000, at the Feira meeting, which marked the end of Portugal's presidency.

The preparation timetable

The UK's first changeover plan was published in February 1999 and subsequently refined in March 2000. The plan is one of 'prepare and decide', that is, many of the preparations will be started before the decision to join is actually taken. According to the plan, the government committed itself to prepare to join the euro, with 'tens of millions of pounds' reportedly being spent. Each government department, in many of which work has already begun in earnest, is overseen by a minister.

Public sector planning has included the National Health Service, which has produced its own outline changeover plans. William Hague, the opposition leader, has claimed that such preparation without a commitment to join is a waste of money, and has pledged to stop such work immediately if the Conservative Party is elected.

The changeover plan envisages euro notes and coin being introduced around two/two-and-a-half years after a successful referendum result. The precise date depends on how quickly government and business could convert. According to the UK plan, sterling would be withdrawn from circulation six months after this date. However, since the UK's plan was originally published, the initial eurozone countries have shortened this period of dual circulation from the originally envisaged six months to two months or less. The UK would probably now also opt for such a shorter period.

It is not clear from the changeover plan whether the two-and-a-half-year preparation period is one in which sterling's exchange rate is fixed to the euro. That is, whether the period is similar to the three-year period from 1 January 1999 to 1 January 2002 for the initial euro area members. It may be that part of this period is spent with sterling in the ERM, as a prelude to fixing the sterling-euro conversion factor.

What will euro notes and coin look like?

Euro banknotes will be of denominations of €5, €10, €50, €100, €200 and €500. They feature designs of bridges, arches and tunnels in different architectural styles. For example, the €100 note features a rococo-style arch on the front. The banknotes are of the same design in each country. No national distinguishing features (for example, the Queen's head) are allowed.

The coins are in denominations of 1, 2, 5, 10, 20 and 50 cents and €1 and €2. The have a common design on the front, but each country has its own national designs on the reverse.

For the initial eurozone countries, some 50 billion coins and 14.5 billion notes had to be produced. The Royal Mint and the Bank of England will produce the UK's own supply of notes and coin if the UK joins the euro. Designing the national symbols for the reverse of the coins and then producing the notes and coin will take around two years.

Conclusions

Clearly, the three timetables are heavily dependent upon each other and, by way of conclusion, it is interesting to consider two scenarios (both of which assume a 'Yes' result to a referendum). The first is a rather leisurely approach. This involves the report on Mr Brown's tests being produced at the end of the indicated two-year period and a referendum four months later. UK businesses would then start their preparations which would, in turn, take two and a half years. Then, there would be a two-month period of dual circulation of sterling and the euro. The total time taken would be five years, so the process could just about be completed within one parliamentary term.

At the other extreme, a 'fast track' approach would see Mr Brown's report produced within, say, six months of the election, again with the referendum following on four months later. The period for business preparations could be squeezed down to perhaps two years, followed by two months of dual circulation. The total time taken would thus be around three years.

The fact that sterling has not re-entered the ERM is an obstacle to fulfilling a 'fast track' timetable, as it is likely to slow down EU approval of UK membership. In this sense, very early membership of the ERM would be helpful. After the Labour government was elected in May 1997, one of Gordon Brown's first – and surprising – actions as chancellor, was to give the Bank of England greater independence in setting interest rates. Should he be returned as the next chancellor, then he may be considering rejoining the ERM as his next surprise.

12

The changeover in the retail sector

If the UK decides to join the euro, then there will clearly be a period of preparation, during which all sectors of the economy will face challenges. However, it would arguably be the retail sector which would require the greatest modifications to adopt the euro. Naturally, such an upheaval has a cost implication and experience from the first wave of euro countries shows that the costs of preparation are indeed the highest in this sector of the economy. Moreover, for some members of the general public, the retail sector may provide the first direct exposure to the euro on their first shopping trip after 'E-Day'.

By joining the euro later than other countries, the potential problems and costs are, to some extent, reduced. For example, by the time the UK could join the euro, many consumers would at least have had some experience of euro notes and coin through travel to eurozone countries. They are also likely to have a general idea of the exchange rate between sterling and the euro, not least because this is widely reported. In addition, UK retailers may also have gleaned some knowledge from the experience of retailers in other European countries. Finally, the changeover period in the UK is likely to be shorter than it was in the founder euro-area countries – perhaps one to two years, rather than the three that they experienced.

The most important period for the retail sector's preparations would run from the time when a fixed conversion rate between sterling and the euro is announced to the time at which euro notes and coin replaced sterling.

The conversion rate between sterling and the euro would, in keeping with EU regulations, be set to six significant figures. It is most unlikely to be a round number.

12-1

Euro prices: up, down, or unchanged?

Example of £1/€ conversion factor
€1 = £0.798635

UK retailer: T-shirt pricing

Prices unchanged

	£ prices		€ prices
Example #1	Original price: **£4.99**	*Equivalent to:* →	€6.25

Prices rounded up

	£ prices		€ prices
	Original price: **£4.99**	*Equivalent to:* →	€6.25
Example #2			Could be changed to: ↓
★ *New price*: **£5.58**	← *Equivalent to:*		€6.99

Prices rounded down

	£ prices		€ prices
	Original price: **£4.99**	*Equivalent to:* →	€6.25
Example #3			Could be changed to: ↓
★ *New price:* £4.78	← *Equivalent to:*		€5.99

For example, the UK could have a conversion factor of :

$$1 \text{ euro} = £ 0.798635$$

This conversion rate would be used for converting all sterling prices into euro and vice versa. An article priced at £4.99, say, would thus have an equivalent price of 6.25 euros (see Figure 12-1). In the UK, it is common for retail outlets to quote prices at one penny under a round figure, say £4.99, £9.99 or whatever. This practice, which is designed to makes goods appear relatively cheap (even though the saving is a mere 1p), is widespread. It is doubtful that a change to euro pricing would alter this pricing strategy and so the critical question is whether retailers would

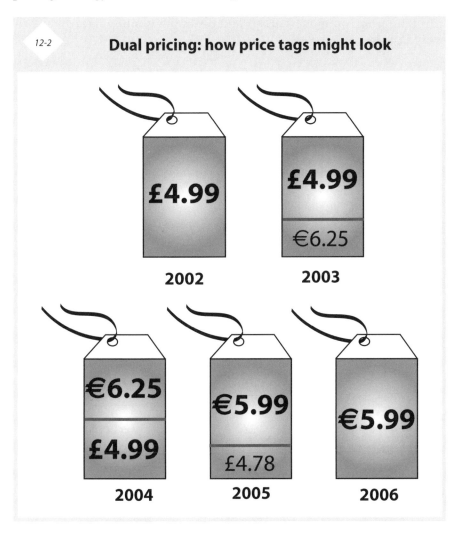

Dual pricing: how price tags might look

12-2

round converted prices up, say, from 6.25 euros to 6.99 euros or round down to 5.99 euros. This is critical, not just for the purses of the consumer, but also for high street inflation. In the example just quoted, the rounding up results in a price hike of 12 per cent, while the rounding down results in a saving of 4 per cent.

It is possible – for some goods, at least – to correct for conversion by making compensating changes in quantity (e.g. the Mars® bar could be become bigger, while the loaf of bread could be reduced in size). Even so, there is a potential for some significant changes in the relative prices of different goods which, in turn, could have substantial effects on the pattern of consumption. Furthermore, there is also a risk of consumer confusion. The situation has been likened to that following decimalization in the UK, when there was widespread concern that changing from 'pounds, shillings and pence' to 'pounds and new pence' would push prices up.

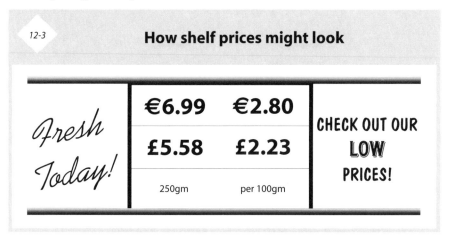

12-3   **How shelf prices might look**

Fresh Today!	€6.99	€2.80	CHECK OUT OUR
	£5.58	£2.23	LOW
	250gm	per 100gm	PRICES!

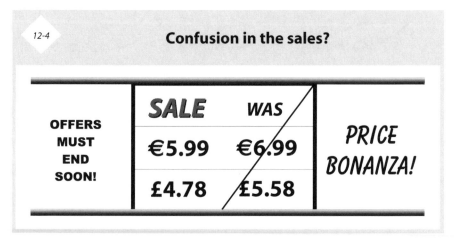

12-4   **Confusion in the sales?**

OFFERS MUST END SOON!	SALE	WAS	PRICE
	€5.99	€6.99	BONANZA!
	£4.78	£5.58	

This concern over higher prices is compounded by the fact that the costs of changing over to the euro are likely to be high for retail outlets. The financial burdens to be faced include:

- dual pricing – the longer prices are expressed in two currencies, the greater the costs;
- staff training to prepare for the new currency;
- handling of two currencies for the period when they circulate side-by-side (expected to be about two months);
- installation of new systems, cash tills etc. to accommodate the euro.

Various estimates of the costs have been made. Marks & Spencer, for example, puts the cost of installing all the new systems and technology *alone* at £100 million. If one scales up the M&S figure for the entire UK retail sector, a total cost of £2bn or €2.5bn (at an exchange rate of 80 pence per euro) is implied. Since the M&S figure is solely for technical costs, and excludes the extraneous items mentioned above, such as staff training, it should be viewed as a rather conservative estimate. For example, Eurocommerce, which represents retailers throughout the EU, estimates the costs to be 1.8 % to 2.5% of turnover. This figure implies a cost for UK retailers of some €6.7 to €8.3 billion

Given the costly nature of the changeover, the obvious issue is whether it is worth it? There are two ways of looking at this question. Certainly, at

the parochial level, the answer lies in calculating whether the upheaval can be outweighed by the potential benefits – at least for consumers – arising from greater price transparency, greater competition in retailing and a possible reduction in prices. Meanwhile, the retailers themselves have to assess not only whether the costs of conversion can recouped,. but also whether the euro will bring increased profitability. Secondly, both consumers and retailers have to view this inconvenience and cost in the light of the wider impact (e.g. interest rates) which moving to the euro will entail.

Conclusion

For both the consumer and the retailer, any transition from sterling to euro prices would not be painless. The fact that the UK would be joining the euro later than other countries would certainly help to reduce transition costs, but these would nevertheless be substantial. Moreover, the costs are up-front, in that they must be met before any benefits accrue. Such benefits are not tangible, cannot be quantified, and may take some time to materialize.

13

Staying outside

The aim of this chapter is to explore the issues involved in the UK staying outside the euro-area. We place emphasis not on the immediate, but rather the longer-term, consequences.

How isolated would the UK be?

If the UK does not join the euro, it would share that status with, at most, two other EU countries: Sweden and Denmark. Sweden, like the UK, has yet to decide on the issue. Denmark, meanwhile, has voted against membership in a referendum (although there is always the chance of a second referendum being held).

After the euro has been introduced as a currency in circulation in January 2002, the next main project for the EU will be the inclusion of new member countries. There are thirteen candidate countries: Bulgaria, Cyprus, the Czech Republic, Estonia, Hungary, Latvia, Lithuania, Malta, Poland, Romania, Slovakia, Slovenia and Turkey.

These countries will not have, like the UK and Denmark, an 'opt-out' from the euro. In joining the EU, they will agree to implement all of the provisions of the various Treaties governing the operation of the EU. That effectively means that they agree also to join the euro. However, it does not mean that the instant they join the euro they will become members of the euro-area. Rather, their currencies will have to spend two years in the Exchange Rate Mechanism, and they will need to meet the EU's convergence criteria before they could adopt the single currency. However, almost all of the candidate countries are very keen to join the euro as soon as possible – and many are also in a good position to meet the convergence requirements, even before joining the EU. Furthermore, some have even expressed a desire to join the euro *before* joining the EU. Effectively, two countries – Estonia and Bulgaria – have done this already as they have pegged their currencies to the euro. (This is done through a

13-1

Test 1: government deficit

EMU countries

Other EU countries

First Wave countries

Second Wave countries

'currency board' arrangement, which means that their domestic currency is backed by official holdings of euro.)

As many as ten of the candidate countries (that is all bar Bulgaria, Romania and Turkey, which are further behind the rest in the process of economic reform) could join the EU in 2004-2005. There will be a further wave of expansion, maybe two or three years after that.

In the next ten years or so, there is a reasonable chance of the euro-area incorporating twenty or more countries and, with the overwhelming majority of EU countries also being in the euro-area, the UK may be increasingly isolated if it does not join the euro.

Life outside the euro-area

In such circumstances, what would be the implications of remaining out?

UK excluded from ECB and EuroGroup decisions

The UK would obviously be excluded from ECB decisions if it did not join the euro. It would also be excluded from the meetings of the group of euro-area finance ministers, referred to as the 'Eurogroup'. However, would this be a particularly bad thing? The ECB's Governing Council currently comprises six members of the Executive Board and the 12 governors of the national central banks. With the planned expansion of the euro-area, there is a real risk that the difficulties the one-size-fits-all approach to interest rates would take on truly monumental proportions.

Furthermore, since not being a part of the ECB would allow the UK to continue to control its interest rates, it is possible that such 'isolation' could actually be a major benefit.

Two other European countries would be outside the EU and the euro

Two other European countries – Switzerland and Norway – would be outside both the EU and the euro-area. If Denmark and Sweden also remained out, there would be five countries – all of them prosperous by average European standards – outside the euro-area. Furthermore, the UK has a closer relationship with North America than do most other countries.

UK companies could use the euro

Whatever the future, UK companies would still be free to use the euro as a currency. There is no prohibition on the use of the euro in the UK. One example serves to show how developments on this front may actually be quite unusual. In March 1998, shortly before the initial members of the euro-area were selected, the EU's economic and finance ministers met in York (the UK had the presidency of the EU at the time). The *Yorkshire Post* interviewed representatives of local industry to canvass opinion on what the euro would mean. Rowntree, the biggest employer, stated that the euro would be of great importance for them from the moment it was launched: they would be using it in their internal accounting systems and administrative functions. The news no doubt surprised many *Yorkshire Post* readers, but the explanation was straightforward. Rowntree, was owned by Nestlé, a Swiss company which was itself intending to use the euro from soon after its January 1999 launch. In this way, the UK subsidiary of a Swiss company found itself immediately exposed to the euro.

Such examples are set to become quite common. UK firms engaged in pan-European trade may find that they will want – or will be encouraged - to conduct a large part of their business in euro rather than sterling.

Is the euro just another foreign currency?

It can be argued that many UK companies are quite familiar with dealing in currencies other than sterling and that the euro can be treated as 'just another' foreign currency. To some extent that is true, but the euro is set to be much more significant to the UK than any other currency, accounting for the largest part of the UK's overseas trade.

The disadvantages of using two currencies

Many companies may find they operate predominantly in just two currencies – sterling and euro. This is undoubtedly feasible, but will entail extra costs: two bank accounts, two accounting systems, the exposure to shifts in the sterling-euro exchange rate or the costs of hedging such exposure.

It would be simpler to use just one currency. Moreover, if it is likely that the UK will eventually join the euro, then it would be sensible to do it sooner rather than later. There will be costs in switching over no matter when the UK joins, but the sooner it joins the sooner the benefits of using just one currency will begin.

ERM as a halfway house

Stability of sterling against the euro would go some way towards helping companies adjust to the UK being outside the euro. This could be achieved if the UK joined the ERM, but this would need to be with fluctuation bands that were narrower than the standard 15% if substantial gains in terms of exchange rate stability were to be obtained – Denmark partially compensates for being out of the euro by having relatively tight 2.25% bands against the euro. There would, however, always be a risk for sterling that, given the UK's previous ERM experience, any such bands would not be regarded as very binding.

Conclusions

Staying out of the euro is an option, but it is one which would see the UK increasingly isolated, with more countries likely to join the euro-area in coming years. However, as we have noted, the expansion of the euro-area could bring with it a new set of problems, not least the dilution of member states influence over economic policy. In the meantime, companies would be free to operate in euro and, no doubt, many will do this. For some, that will involve the costs of using two currencies side by side. If the UK does seem likely to join the euro eventually, then there would seem little point in delaying the event, since the transition costs will have to borne no matter when the UK joins. However, any perceived benefits would be missed for the duration of the UK's delay in entering. For companies concerned about exchange rate volatility, rejoining the ERM could provide an important safety net.

14

Is there a way out?

Many would feel more comfortable about the UK joining the euro if there was an obvious 'way out'. This chapter explores:

- The legal position on leaving the euro;
- The reasons the UK might want to leave in the future; and
- The pressures which might bring about a break-up of the euro.

Legally, there is no way out

If the UK joined the euro, then sterling would legally be replaced by the euro as the currency of the UK once the rate between sterling and the euro was locked. (In the founder eleven countries that happened on 1 January 1999.) When sterling is withdrawn from circulation and replaced by euro notes and coin, sterling will also lose its legal tender status.

There is no legal provision for a country leaving the euro – no 'exit clause' has been agreed in advance. Arguably, such a provision might encourage countries to join in a half-hearted way, knowing there was an obvious way out, but that is precisely the reason there is no such provision.

However, although there is no apparent legal method to leave, it could still happen. An historical precedent lies in the Baltic States: when they seceded from the USSR, one of their first actions was to establish their own central bank and issue their own currency. Nevertheless, just as the preparations to join the euro will take several years, any new UK currency could not be launched overnight. Legally, and practically, it would not be possible to revert to using sterling, since it would no longer exist, while notes and coin would have been removed from circulation. Reference to sterling in all contracts would have been superseded by a reference to the euro, with the euro replacing sterling at the fixed conversion rate.

A new UK currency, distinct from the 'old sterling' would be needed. A conversion rate for euro into 'new sterling' would then need to be set and the institutions to deal with its issue would have to be created. The process is likely to be just as time consuming and costly as the original switch from sterling into the euro.

Why the UK might want to leave

The UK might want to leave the euro-area for a number of reasons. For example, the 'one-size-fits-all' approach to interest rates might lead to rates being set at a level which is manifestly wrong for the UK economy. If this were just a temporary problem, it may be tolerated – but if it continued for a number of years, and if it proved difficult to use other methods of controlling the economy, pressures to leave the euro would intensify. Alternatively, disagreements about management of the euro-area, especially as it incorporates more countries, could intensify.

The breakdown of fixed currency relationships does not, of course, normally take place in an environment of calm contemplation about whether the level of interest rates is 'right' or 'wrong', or whether a country would be better 'in' or 'out'. Any currency breakdown is invariably a crisis, with unwanted speculative attacks usually rubbing salt into the wound.

In this light, where are the areas of vulnerability? And how might these result in pressures which would force the UK to leave the euro, even if this were against the UK's wishes? Note that all should be regarded as risks, rather than likely projections.

Pressures which might force the UK out

1: Speculative attack on sterling during ERM membership

If the UK re-entered the ERM as a preparation for joining the euro, sterling could be vulnerable to speculative attack. Financial markets might consider the UK to have entered at (for example) too strong a rate against the euro. Speculative pressures could force sterling out of the ERM and this would disqualify the UK from euro-area membership. Effectively, this would result in sterling being forced out of the running before the UK had formally joined the euro.

2: Pressures once the sterling-euro conversion rate has been set

There would also be risks once the conversion rate to the euro had been set, that is to say, the period immediately after ERM membership. Pressures in this period could first manifest themselves within the UK banking system. For example, if there was concern that the UK could pull out of the euro, the status of euro-denominated bank deposits with UK banks would be called into question. What would happen to these if the UK came out? Would they still be repaid in euro? Or would they be converted into sterling? Depositors might prefer to switch to a bank in a country that was a more committed euro-area member. This would undermine the credibility of UK banks and could potentially lead to a massive capital outflow from the UK.

3: Difficulty of dealing with shocks

There are significant concerns as to whether the convergence amongst the euro-area countries is strong enough to avoid possible shocks. The ability to cope with shocks as a member of the euro-area is one of Mr Brown's tests of whether it is appropriate for the UK to join. However, as we noted in Chapter 6, history shows that the UK does not respond to shocks in the same way as other euro-area countries. Of course, these shocks are, by their very nature, unpredictable and neither the form nor magnitude of future shocks can be foreseen.

4: Political problems

With so much political capital invested in the euro project, the chances of a politically-induced rupture in the initial years seem to be small. Nonetheless, the well-publicized difficulties over the ECB presidency, for example, highlight the divisions over euro-area policy. Adverse economic conditions could push these tensions to breaking point.

5: Contagion

The risks of the UK leaving need not be triggered by developments in the UK. They may just as easily be set off by developments in other euro-area countries. Financial market crises in recent years have been characterized by 'contagion', with problems in one country spilling over to countries which may seem only loosely-connected.

For example, suppose a country in the euro-area started to break the rules on the size of its budget deficit. Moreover, assume that it showed no signs of remedying the situation, and that it faced paying ever-higher rates of interest to finance its borrowing. This situation could easily reach a point where there was genuine concern that the country could default. The Maastricht Treaty does contain a safeguard which ensures that a country could not be bailed out by other euro-area countries in such circumstances. But there is concern that, despite this safeguard, any such scenario would cause the credibility of the entire euro-area to be called into question. One country's problems might easily spread to others and those countries seen as least committed to the euro would be the most vulnerable.

6: Perception and historic precedent

Three European monetary unions have been formed in the past, but each has eventually broken down. This historic precedent leads to some to hold the perceive that a future breakdown will be inevitable.

France, Italy, Belgium, Switzerland and Greece formed the Latin Monetary Union in 1865. Each country maintained its own currency, tying it to that of its neighbours with a fixed exchange rate of 1:1. Only gold and silver coins were included in the union, since, at that time, the use of banknotes was relatively limited and it was partly for this reason that there was no central bank. As a result of the absence of such an institution, each country was responsible for the issuance of its own currency and this led to a number of abuses. Italy, for example, created inflation by issuing an excessive amount of banknotes which were not fully backed by gold. In addition, the large number of different coins in circulation meant that it was difficult for consumers and merchants to distinguish between them, and widespread confusion resulted. The First World War exacerbated the tensions in the system and the union finally broke down in 1926. Two other monetary unions were also formed in the nineteenth century. The Scandinavian monetary union (formed in 1872) linked the currencies of Denmark, Sweden and the Norway together with 1:1 exchange rates. The German monetary union (formed in 1838) linked the currencies of the North German Confederation, the Kingdom of Bavaria and the Austro-Hungarian Empire. Both unions also collapsed after the First World War.

Of course, financial systems today are much more sophisticated than those of the early twentieth century. However, whether that attribute is a safeguard or a risk is not obvious.

Conclusions

Legally, there is no way out of the euro and so, if the UK joins, it should be regarded as an irreversible action. In extreme circumstances, the UK could choose to leave, but the process of leaving and re-establishing a new currency would be complex, not least because reverting to 'old sterling' would not be possible.

Market pressures might force the UK to leave in certain circumstances. None of these should be considered as very likely – rather, they are conceivable longer-term risks. However, if the euro-area countries and institutions are aware of the risks and are vigilant in preventing them developing, then the euro-area will be more durable.

15

Conclusions

Joining the euro would be an extremely important step for the UK. Everyone would be affected. The consequences of replacing sterling with the euro are far-reaching and need to be carefully weighed. This book has attempted to provide a balanced view of the issues involved.

If the UK does decide to join the euro, then the first step will be to have a fixed rate which links the value of sterling to the euro. This would be similar to the fixed exchange rates which the UK has had in the past. The significant difference is that it would be 'irrevocable', acting as a stepping- stone to eventual replacement of sterling with the euro. This would happen around two years later.

There is nothing new about the UK having a fixed exchange rate with another currency. But in the past each of the linkages the UK has had to other currencies has eventually broken down. The explanation for the breakdown has invariably been a conflict between what was needed to maintain the exchange rate link and what was needed for the domestic economy. This tension is likely to exist if sterling joins the euro. Indeed, the 'one-size-fits-all approach to interest rates in the euro-area is the biggest disadvantage to the UK joining. There are also significant costs involved in the changeover.

Joining the euro will not happen overnight. In the UK, there will be an assessment of Gordon Brown's tests followed, if this is favourable, by a vote in parliament and a referendum. The EU also has to decide if the UK satisfies the five 'convergence requirements'. The UK easily passes four of these: indeed, it is in a significantly stronger position than the existing euro-area members. The fifth requirement – that the UK must re-enter the Exchange Rate Mechanism (ERM) – is trickier. Re-entering would undoubtedly rekindle memories of Black Wednesday (16 September 1992) when huge foreign exchange speculation, resulted in the UK abandoning its ERM link to the Deutschemark. The ERM has been reformed (it is now 'ERM II'), but the potential pressures on sterling remain.

The UK would want to join at the 'right' exchange rate. There is no single answer to what that right rate is, but we suggest it is around 80 pence to one euro. There is thus an issue relating to how sterling's exchange rate can be managed to such a weaker level.

There is no guarantee that even if Mr. Brown's tests and the EU's tests were satisfied, and the exchange rate was right, that joining the euro would be the correct decision. The flexible and competitive nature of the UK economy compares favourably with the euro-area. The openness and transparency of the Bank of England also compare favourably with the ECB.

If the UK joins the euro, the transition from sterling to euro for the consumer is unlikely to be straightforward. The fact that the UK is joining the euro later than other countries may help to reduce the transition costs but these are still expected to be substantial. The costs, moreover, are easy to identify and will be required before the expected benefits accrue.

These benefits are expected to be substantial. Exchange rate stability would undoubtedly be very welcome in many areas of the economy. Consumers, as well as companies, would benefit from an easier comparison of costs and prices. Interest rates may be lower and the financial markets would probably be more efficient and liquid.

Staying out of the euro is, of course, an option. But it is one which would see the UK increasingly isolated, with more countries likely to join the euro area in coming years. UK companies would be free to operate in euro and many will do this. But using sterling and the euro side-by-side will entail extra costs.

Legally, there is no 'way out' of the euro if the UK joins. It should be regarded as irreversible. In extreme circumstances, the UK could choose to leave – or even be forced to leave – but that process would be just as complex, costly and time-consuming as joining the euro in the first place.

Glossary

convergence requirements

In order to join the euro the UK must satisfy the EU's five convergence requirements, relating to the government's budget deficit, stock of government debt, inflation rate, bond yield and exchange rate stability (see Chapter 7).

conversion factor

All currencies that are members of the euro-area have a conversion factor between their national currencies and the euro. For the original eleven euro-area countries these became effective on 1 January 1999. There will be a fixed conversion factor between sterling and the euro which is used before sterling notes and coin are finally replaced with the euro. This will probably be shorter than three years. The UK government changeover plan suggests it will last two and a half years.

For the original eleven countries these conversion factors were expressed to six significant figures (e.g. one euro equals 1.95583 Deutschemarks). There would be a similar conversion factor for sterling, for example:

$$1 \text{ euro} = £\ 0.798635$$

ECB (European Central Bank)

The ECB is the central bank, located in Frankfurt, Germany which sets the interest rate for the countries of the euro-area.

European Monetary Institute (EMI)

The EMI was a temporary institution established at the start of Stage Two of EMU, on 1 January 1994. The two main tasks of the EMI were:

(i) to strengthen central bank co-operation and monetary policy co-ordination, and

(ii) to make the preparations for the establishment of the ECB.

It went into liquidation when the ECB was formed on 1 June 1998.

Ecu (European Currency Unit)

The Ecu was a basket of made up of fixed amounts of 12 of the 15 countries of the EU. The Ecu was replaced by the euro on a one-to-one basis on 1 January 1999.

euro

The name of the European currency adopted by the *European Council* at its meeting in Madrid on 15 and 16 December 1995, and used instead of the term Ecu which was used in the *Maastricht Treaty*.

euro-area *or* eurozone

The two terms are used interchangeably. The euro-area or eurozone comprises those countries in which the euro has been adopted as the single currency and in which a single monetary policy is conducted by the *Governing Council* of the *European Central Bank (ECB)*.

The euro-area comprises Austria, Belgium, Finland, France, Germany, Greece, Ireland, Italy, Luxembourg, the Netherlands, Portugal and Spain.

European Commission

The European Commission is the European Union institution that takes the initiatives for EU policies, proposes EU legislation and exercises powers in certain areas. It consists of 20 members and includes two nationals from Germany, Spain, France, Italy and the United Kingdom, and one from each of the other member countries.

European Council

The European Council comprises the heads of state or government of the member states of the European Union. European Council meetings are referred to as summits. They take place at least twice a year, normally at the end of a country's presidency of the EU. For example, the Nice summit took place at the end of France's presidency in the second half of 2000.

European Parliament

There are 626 members of the European Parliament representing the citizens of the member countries of the EU. The Maastricht Treaty establishes certain procedures for the democratic accountability of the ECB to the European Parliament. For example, ECB officials give evidence at hearings of various parliamentary committees.

European Union

The European Union has 15 member countries: Austria, Belgium, Denmark, Finland, France, Germany, Greece, Ireland, Italy, Luxembourg, the Netherlands, Portugal, Spain, Sweden and the UK.

Eurostat

The body responsible for the production of EU statistics.

Economic and Monetary Union (EMU)

European Economic and Monetary Union covers both *economic union* – the free movement of goods, labour and capital within the EU - and *monetary union* – the use of the euro.

The achievement of EMU has taken place in three stages:

- **Stage One** of EMU started in July 1990 and ended on 31 December 1993. The main feature of this stage was the removal of barriers to free capital movements within the EU. Prior to that, many countries had restrictions of capital flows.

- **Stage Two** of EMU began on 1 January 1994. In this stage the *European Monetary Institute (EMI)* was established, preparing for the launch of the ECB and the euro.

- **Stage Three** started on 1 January 1999, with the launch of the *euro*.

ERM and ERM II

The Exchange Rate Mechanism was originally designed as a way of limiting exchange rate movements of European currencies against each other. Up until 1993, fluctuation bands of either plus or minus 2.25% or plus or minus 6% were allowed against a currency's central rate against the other member currencies of the ERM. When sterling was a member from 1990 to 1992, it was with a central rate against the Deutschemark of DM2.95/£ and 6% bands. Each currency's central rate was used as the basis for its *conversion factor* against the euro.

When the euro was launched on 1 January 1999, a new version of the ERM, ERM II, came into operation. Membership is voluntary for those EU countries which have not joined the euro. Greece was a member until it joined the euro on 1 January 2001. Denmark is the only current member.

Sterling would almost certainly need to be a member of ERM II for two years before being able to join the euro. The choice of the central rate against the euro when sterling joins will be of great importance as this is likely to form the basis of the eventual conversion factor between sterling and the euro. Sterling is likely to enter with the normal bands of plus or minus 15% (Denmark unilaterally opted for narrower, 2.25% bands).

G7 countries

The Group of Seven countries comprises Canada, France, Germany, Italy, Japan, the UK and the USA.

Governing Council

This is the main decision-making body of the *European Central Bank (ECB)*. It comprises all the members of the Executive Board of the ECB and the governors of the national central banks of the countries that have adopted the euro. This is the body that sets interest rates for the euro-area.

General Council

The General Council one of the governing bodies of the *European Central Bank (ECB)*. It comprises the president and the vice-president of the ECB and the governors of all 15 EU national central banks. This body has largely administrative responsibilities and does not set interest rates for the euro-area.

inflation target

A target for the rate of inflation. The UK target is currently set by the UK Treasury and is for a rate of inflation of 2.5%. The inflation rate should be within plus or minus 1% of that rate. The measure of inflation used is the Retail Prices Index, excluding mortgage interest payments (normally referred to as RPIX).

The ECB's inflation target is that inflation should be less than 2%. The ECB itself sets the inflation target. The measure of inflation used is the rate of increase in the Harmonized Consumer Price Index *(HCPI) for* all of the twelve countries in the euro-area set by either the government or the central bank.

Louvre Accord

The agreement by the *G7* countries, made on 22 February 1987, that their currencies were within ranges broadly consistent with economic fundamentals and that they should aim for broad stability of exchange rates.

Maastricht Treaty

The Maastricht Treaty was signed in Maastricht on 7 February 1992 and entered into force on 1 November 1993 after it had been ratified by each of the EU member states. It sets out the main requirements for entering into *Economic and Monetary Union (EMU)*.

monetary aggregates

A monetary aggregate is defined as the sum of currency in circulation plus certain other liabilities of financial institutions. The ECB has target for the growth of M3, a broad measure of the money supply. It includes: currency in circulation; euro-area residents' holdings of bank deposits with an agreed maturity of up to two years and deposits redeemable at notice with a maturity of up to three months; repurchase agreements; money market fund shares/units; money market paper; and debt securities with a maturity of up to two years.

The *ECB* sets a 'reference rate' for the growth of M3. This has been 4.5% per year since 1999.

Plaza Accord

The agreement between France, Germany, Japan, the UK and the USA reached at the Plaza hotel in New York on 22 September 1985. These countries agreed that the US dollar was overvalued and that a further fall in its value would be desirable.

price stability

Price stability technically means prices that are stable, i.e. do not change over time. It is the formal aim of the ECB. In practice, mainly because of the difficulty of measuring average prices, the aim of price stability is usually taken to mean a low rate of inflation (i.e. a low rate of increase in the price level) such as 2% per year.

Notes

Chapter 1: Introduction

- The fixed conversion factors are widely publicized and can be found, for example, on the European Central bank's website, www.ecb.int.

Chapter 2: Sterling: a brief history

- For a description of the events leading to the choice of the conversion rate between sterling and gold see Chapter 12 *The Great Recoinage and the Last of the Magicians* in Peter L. Bernstein's book, *The Power of Gold* (Wiley, 2000).
- For a more lighthearted version of these events, I am grateful to my daughter for pointing out the chapter *The Forger's Nightmare* in *Isaac Newton and his apple*, by Kjartan Poskitt (Hippo books, 1999).
- See also David Sinclair, *The Pound: a biography* (Arrow books, 2000).
- A lively account of the history of fixing exchange rates can be found in Alan Walters, *Sterling in Danger* (Fontana, 1990).
- Ziegler's comment on the 1967 devaluation is taken from Philip Ziegler's, *Wilson* (Weidenfeld and Nicolson, 1993) page 282.
- For a detailed discussion of the events leading up to the formation of the Bretton Woods system see the third volume of Robert Skidelsky's biography of J M Keynes: *John Maynard Keynes: Fighting for Britain, 1937-1946* (Macmillan, 2000) pp 337-372.
- See Paul Temperton, *A Guide to UK Monetary Policy* (Macmillan, 1985) and Paul Temperton, *UK Monetary Policy: the challenge for the 1990s* (Macmillan, 1990) for a description of the monetary policies that wee conducted in the 1980s.
- A detailed discussion of the ERM crisis in 1992/93 can be found in Paul Temperton's (ed.) *The European Currency Crisis* (Probus, 1993)

Chapter 3: The euro: an even briefer history

- A detailed discussion if the process leading to the fixing of the euro conversion factors, their relationship with the ERM central rates and the Ecu-euro conversion is contained in Chapter 4 *'How the euro is being created'* by Pat McArdle in Paul Temperton's (ed.) *The euro* (2nd. edition, Wiley, 1998).

Chapter 4: What will the UK gain by joining the euro?

- The McKinsey study which is cited was quoted in *'Price is right for most companies despite the euro'*, by Peter Marsh in the *Financial Times*, 4 August 1999.

Chapter 5: What will the UK lose by joining the euro?

- The average costs quoted for the changeover come from the Association for the Monetary Union of Europe's newsletter *European Monetary Union for Business*, June 2000.

Chapter 6: Does the euro pass Mr Brown's tests?

- The IMF study on growth correlations is reported in the IMF's *World Economic Outlook*, October 1997, pp 62-63.
- The IMF study also updated the estimates of the response of different European economies to economic shocks which were first made by Bayoumi and Eichengreen. These were reported in *'Shocking Aspects of European Monetary Unification'* in *Adjustment and Growth in the European Monetary Union*, Francisco Torres & Francesco Giavazzi (eds.) (Cambridge University Press, 1993).
- Britain in Europe's estimates of the job losses from being outside the euro were reported in an article entitled *'Up to 66,000 jobs lost outside the euro'* in the *Financial Times*, 31 December 2001.

Chapter 7: Does the UK pass the EU's tests

- The convergence criteria are set out in *Treaty on European Union* (Office for Official Publications of the European Community, 1992).

Chapter 8: What is the right exchange rate for joining the euro?

- The most recent estimate of FEERS (fundamental equilibrium exchange rates) was produced by the Institute for International Economics in late 1998 in *Fundamental Equilibrium Exchange rates for 2000*, a summary of which is available on their website, www.iie.com. The estimates FEER for sterling against the euro is derived from their FEERs for the DM/£ of around DM2.34/£ or 84 pence per euro.

Chapter 9: Are two tests enough?

- The IoDs tests were reported in the IoD's euro tests *'would rule out early entry'* *Financial Times*, 17 August 1999.
- The IMD data on international competitiveness come from The International Institute for Management Development, *see* www.imd.ch
- The data on business start-ups come from the Kauffman Center, quoted in the *Financial Times*, Tuesday June 22 1999
- The data on UK regional differences come from *Regional Trends*, no. 35, (The Stationery Office).

Chapter 10: The Bank of England and the ECB

- Biographical information on the members of the Bank of England's Monetary Policy Committee can be found on the Bank's website, www.bankofengland.co.uk. Biographical information on the ECB board members can be found on www.ecb.int.

Chapter 11: The road ahead

- For a description of the preparations taking place in the UK see *'Chapter 4: Preparations for Possible UK entry'* in the Bank of England publication, *Practical issues arising from the euro* (November 2000).

Chapter 12: The changeover in the retail sector

- The examples given on dual pricing are based on a range of different experiences of the retail sector. A good guide for retailers is the *Euro preparation guide for retailers*, produced by the Association for the Monetary Union of Europe, *see* www.amue.org.

Chapter 13: Staying outside

- A description of the issues surrounding the UK not joining the euro was given in a Centre for Economic Policy Research seminar by Willem Buiter, entitled *'The Risks of being outside: Britain and EMU'*, on 2 July 1998. This chapter draws on the arguments presented in that seminar.

Chapter 14: Is there a way out?

- For a description of the break-up of previous monetary unions see *'History offers a pertinent lesson'* by Luca Einaudi in the *Financial Times*, 26 February 1999.

- For a more detailed description of the legal provisions surrounding the euro, see Cliff Dammers' *'The euro: eliminating legal uncertainty'* in Paul Temperton's (ed.) *The euro* (2nd edition, Wiley, 1998).

Index